Jacob's Encounters With GOD

The Beginning of Israel

Jacob's Encounters With GOD

The Beginning of Israel

Vinu V Das

Tabor Press

ISBN 978-0-9940194-3-1

Table of Contents

Introduction

The story of Jacob is one of the most pivotal narratives in the Bible, marking the transformation of a man into a nation—Israel. His encounters with God shaped his destiny and laid the foundation for the people who would bear his name. These divine moments were not just historical events but spiritual milestones, rich with meaning for believers today.

Jacob's encounters with God, whether through dreams, or direct wrestling with the divine, reveal a pattern of God's relentless pursuit and transformative power. Each of these encounters was intentional, serving a distinct purpose in Jacob's spiritual journey. From his dream at Bethel, where he first witnessed the ladder connecting heaven and earth, to his wrestling at Peniel, where he was renamed Israel, Jacob's life demonstrates the profound work of God in shaping His chosen ones.

This book explores these encounters in depth, examining their significance in Jacob's life and their lasting impact on the people of Israel. Each chapter delves into the purpose of these divine visitations, the identity of the One who met Jacob, and the spiritual truths that continue to speak to believers today.

Beyond the historical and theological study, this book also highlights the personal application of Jacob's encounters with God. His struggles, fears, failures, and ultimate surrender mirror the spiritual journey of every believer. Through Jacob's experiences, we see how God's grace transforms a deceiver into a patriarch, a wanderer into a worshiper, and a fearful man into one who prevails with God.

Additionally, the appendices explore key theological insights, including Jesus Christ as the true ladder between heaven and earth and the mysterious Angel of the Lord who appeared to Jacob. These sections provide a broader understanding of God's redemptive plan, connecting Jacob's story to the greater revelation of Christ.

Jacob's journey is more than ancient history—it is a powerful testimony of how God calls, refines, and establishes His people. As you read through this book, may you be encouraged to seek your own divine encounters, wrestle with God in faith, and embrace the transformation He desires for your life.

1. Jacob's Encounters and Beginning of Israel

From Jacob to Israel: A Journey of Transformation and Covenant Promise

From the earliest chapters of the Old Testament, the Bible recounts stories of ordinary people who, by God's grace and calling, participate in extraordinary events leading to the fulfillment of His divine purpose. Among these figures, Jacob stands out as a pivotal character. He is the son of Isaac and the grandson of Abraham—men with whom God established a covenant that promised blessings, land, and countless descendants. Yet for all the promises Jacob inherits, his life is marked by struggles, deceptions, and personal growth that eventually culminate in a new name: Israel. This new identity foreshadows the birth of a nation set apart for God. Understanding Jacob's journey is not just about studying history; it illuminates the greater narrative of redemption that God is weaving throughout the Scriptures. By exploring Jacob's life, we gain deeper insight into the nature of God—His mercy, His patience, and His unwavering commitment to fulfill His promises despite human frailty.

Jacob's story spans multiple chapters in the Book of Genesis, revealing a man who is sometimes cunning and calculating, and at other times humble and reverent before God. He is a man molded by family dynamics, shaped by cultural expectations, and refined through divine encounters. Although he sometimes attempts to manipulate blessings and promises to his advantage, Jacob's path takes him from being a man on the run to becoming the father of the twelve tribes of Israel. His narrative reminds us that God's favor rests not on human perfection but on divine sovereignty and grace. As we walk through the significant moments in Jacob's story let us meditate on how God works in and through imperfect people to establish His eternal purposes.

1.1. Israel: The New Name and the Birth of a Nation

When we reach the point in Jacob's life where God renames him "Israel," we encounter a significant turning point—not only for Jacob personally but also for the unfolding story of the people of God. This moment encapsulates the heart of biblical transformation: a once wayward, self-reliant individual is being reshaped to lead a covenant people

Name as Identity in the Ancient World: In the Old Testament, names often carried weighty significance, reflecting the character, destiny, or calling of a person. For Jacob, who was born grasping his brother's heel and later became known for his cunning and self-serving actions, his original name was suggestive of someone who "supplants" or "grasps." He had lived up to that meaning more than once, tricking his brother Esau and even deceiving his aging father Isaac.

By renaming Jacob "Israel," God was proclaiming a new direction and destiny for him. "Israel" is commonly interpreted as "He struggles with God" or "God contends." This shift emphasizes that Jacob's life would no longer be defined by maneuvering and manipulation; rather, it would be marked by divine purpose and covenant relationship. The renaming thus becomes a tangible sign of God's mercy and sovereign choice, despite

Jacob's flawed past.

The Catalyst for National Identity: Though the Old Testament narrative focuses on Jacob's individual transformation, the name "Israel" quickly becomes a corporate identity. From this point forward, the descendants of Jacob's twelve sons are collectively called the "children of Israel" or the "Israelites." In essence, the personal name Jacob bears becomes the banner under which an entire people will unite and grow into a nation.

This transition is vital for understanding how God works on both micro and macro levels:

- **Individual Transformation**: Jacob is changed in character and identity.

- **National Formation**: The family that springs from Jacob's lineage will eventually become a nation set apart for the Lord.

The dual aspect of Jacob's experience—his personal growth and the establishment of a people—mirrors a broader theological truth: God redeems individuals, but He also forms them into communities meant to reflect His glory and fulfill His redemptive plan. This pattern, seen throughout Scripture, affirms that God's blessings extend through families, tribes, and entire nations, and ultimately to the world.

A Covenant Name Rooted in God's Promises: Long before Jacob's name changed, God had extended a covenant to Abraham, promising him innumerable descendants and a special homeland. This covenant was reaffirmed through Isaac and confirmed to Jacob. When the Lord declared Jacob's new name, He was reinforcing the same covenant promises, now placed firmly on the shoulders of this next generation.

Jacob, now Israel, was the instrument through which God would bring about the next phase of His divine plan. Every time Jacob or his descendants heard the name "Israel," they would be reminded of the following truths:

1. **God Is the One Who Calls**: Israel was chosen not because of Jacob's righteousness but because of God's sovereign love and purpose.

2. **God Is Faithful to His Promises**: The Lord's covenant did not fail when Jacob deceived his father, nor when he fled from Esau; God remained steadfast and continued to affirm His word.

3. **God Transforms the Unworthy**: Jacob's new name signaled to him—and to all future generations—that God can redeem and reshape even the most wayward heart for His glory.

Birth of the Twelve Tribes: One of the most practical outworkings of Jacob's new identity is seen in his growing family. By the time he departs from Laban's household, Jacob has children through Leah, Rachel, and their maidservants—resulting in twelve sons and one daughter. These twelve sons each head what would become the twelve tribes of Israel.

This familial expansion marks the initial stage of nation-building in the biblical narrative. While these tribes would later experience both unity and division, triumph and captivity, it is important to see that God's plan to create a people for Himself was already in motion. Over time, these tribes would:

- **Develop Distinct Identities**: Each tribe had its own territory, leaders, and roles in the future monarchy and religious life of Israel.

- **Bear Witness to God's Covenant**: Whether through blessings, conflicts, or divine interventions, the tribes of Israel were a visible reminder of God's promises to Abraham, Isaac, and Jacob.

- **Prepare the Way for the Messiah**: The most significant outcome of the twelve tribes is that they collectively set the stage for the eventual coming of Jesus Christ, the Savior of the world, who was born from the tribe of Judah.

A Name That Echoes Through History: Finally, the importance of Jacob's new name and the birth of the nation of Israel is seen in how frequently the Scriptures recall these events. Throughout the Old and New Testaments, the name "Israel" appears as a constant reminder of God's covenant people. The prophets speak to "the house of Israel," calling them back to faithfulness. The psalmists celebrate the God of Israel. The New Testament authors interpret Israel's experiences to illuminate Christ's role as the ultimate mediator between God and humanity.

Thus, the name "Israel" resonates far beyond a simple change in how one man was addressed. It stands at the core of the biblical narrative, illustrating God's faithfulness, human transformation, and the abiding purpose to bless all nations of the earth. As Christians meditate on Jacob's journey, we recognize that we, too, are summoned into a transformative relationship with the same God. We may come to Him with our wounds and weaknesses, but He clothes us with new names, new hearts, and a new mission in the world—just as He did for Jacob, renamed Israel, the father of a covenant people who would one day welcome the Savior of all.

1.2. Jacob's Encounters with the Angel of God

Jacob had multiple encounters with the Angel of God throughout his life, both in dreams and in-person. The Bible records at least four significant encounters, each marking an important phase in his spiritual journey.

First Encounter – The Dream at Bethel

- **Type of Encounter:** Dream (Genesis 28:10-22)
- **Summary:** While fleeing from Esau, Jacob stopped to sleep in a wilderness and had a dream of a ladder reaching from earth to heaven, with angels ascending and descending.
- **God's Message:**

- God reaffirmed the covenant made with Abraham and Isaac.
- He promised Jacob the land of Canaan and descendants as numerous as the dust of the earth.
- God assured Jacob of His presence: "I am with you and will keep you wherever you go."

- **Jacob's Response:** He named the place Bethel ("House of God") and made a vow to serve God if God protected and provided for him.
- **Significance:** This was Jacob's first personal encounter with God, showing that God was with him even in exile.

Second Encounter – The Angel of God in a Dream at Haran

- **Type of Encounter:** Dream (Genesis 31:10-13)
- **Summary:** While working for Laban, Jacob had a dream where the Angel of God appeared to him. The Angel showed him how God had been multiplying his flocks through spotted and speckled sheep.
- **God's Message:**
  - The Angel said: "I am the God of Bethel, where you anointed the pillar and where you made a vow to Me." (Genesis 31:13)
  - He instructed Jacob to leave Laban's household and return to Canaan.
- **Jacob's Response:** He obeyed and left Haran with his family and possessions.
- **Significance:** This encounter confirmed God's faithfulness to His promise at Bethel. God protected and blessed Jacob, despite Laban's attempts to cheat him.

Third Encounter – Wrestling with the Angel of God at Peniel

- **Type of Encounter:** In-Person (Genesis 32:24-32)
- **Summary:** The night before meeting Esau, Jacob was left alone and wrestled with a "Man" all night. This Man was God in human form.
- **God's Message:**
    - The Angel touched Jacob's hip, dislocating it, demonstrating divine power.
    - Jacob refused to let go until he was blessed.
    - The Angel changed Jacob's name to Israel, meaning "one who struggles with God and prevails."
- **Jacob's Response:** He named the place Peniel ("Face of God"), saying, "I have seen God face to face, and my life is preserved."
- **Significance:** This was a transformational moment for Jacob—he went from self-reliance to full dependence on God. His new name signified a new identity and purpose.

Fourth Encounter – The Angel of God in a Blessing at Bethel

- **Type of Encounter:** In-Person (Genesis 35:9-15)
- **Summary:** After returning to Canaan, God appeared again to Jacob at Bethel and reaffirmed the covenant.
- **God's Message:**
    - Repeated Jacob's new name: Israel.
    - Confirmed the covenant of land and descendants.
    - Promised that kings and nations would come from his lineage.
- **Jacob's Response:** He set up a pillar of stone and worshiped God.
- **Significance:** This encounter sealed Jacob's transformation and established God's covenant with him as a reality.

These encounters shaped Jacob's faith, identity, and destiny, showing how God personally guides, protects, and transforms those He calls.

Jacob's encounters with the Angel of God marked transformational moments in his life, revealing God's guidance, protection, and covenant promises. Each encounter—whether in a dream or in person—shifted Jacob from a man of self-reliance to a man of faith, ultimately shaping him into Israel, the father of God's chosen nation.

If you found this message encouraging, please share it with others who may benefit. God Bless.

2. First Encounter – The Dream at Bethel

Vision of the ladder connecting heaven and earth.

Jacob's dream at Bethel (Genesis 28:10–22) is one of the most important chapters found in the Old Testament. This passage describes Jacob's travels from Beersheba to Haran, and how he stopped for the night when the sun had set. Using a stone for a pillow, he lay down to sleep and encountered a startling vision of a ladder (or stairway) ascending to heaven, with angels going up and down upon it, and the Lord standing above. God then spoke words of promise and reassurance, echoing the divine pledges earlier made to Abraham and Isaac.

This account takes place in a broader historical and familial context. Jacob, having received Isaac's blessing—though shrouded in controversy and trickery—was fleeing from Esau, who was enraged about the stolen blessing. In this moment of vulnerability, stress, and uncertainty, God chose to appear before Jacob. Far from home, alone, and afraid, Jacob did not initiate this divine communication; rather, God graciously condescended and manifested Himself to Jacob in a dream. This dream changed the direction of Jacob's life and reoriented his perspective, not only about his immediate circumstances but also about the covenantal purposes of the Lord.

2.1. What Is the Purpose?

When unpacking the purpose of this encounter, we must consider four key elements: the context (why Jacob was on the run), the purpose (why God appeared in this moment), the message (what God specifically communicated), and the vision (the significance of the ladder and angels). Each of these elements unfolds the deeper meaning of Jacob's experience and how it spoke both to his personal situation and the unfolding story of God's covenant people.

The Context of the Encounter

Jacob was the grandson of Abraham and the son of Isaac. The Abrahamic covenant promised land, offspring, and blessings that would extend to all nations. By the time we reach Jacob's generation, the promise had not yet fully materialized; however, the covenant had been reaffirmed to Isaac. Jacob's mother, Rebekah, received a prophecy while she was pregnant with twins (Genesis 25:23) that the older (Esau) would serve the younger (Jacob). This divine pronouncement set the stage for Jacob's eventual ascendance over his brother.

Despite the prophetic word, Jacob (with encouragement from his mother) resorted to deceptive methods to secure Isaac's blessing. By disguising himself as Esau, Jacob received the paternal blessing intended for his elder brother, angering Esau to the point of murderous intent. Consequently, Jacob fled to Haran, to the household of Laban (Rebekah's brother). At this point, Jacob is estranged from his home, fearful for his life, and uncertain about his future.

Loneliness and Vulnerability: One cannot overstate Jacob's vulnerability at this point in the narrative. He was not traveling with a large retinue or

18

with the blessings of his family's full support; rather, he was a fugitive. Scripture paints a stark picture: Jacob sets out alone, and as night falls, he has no place to stay. He chooses a random spot under the stars, laying his head on a stone for a pillow—a detail that symbolizes his utter isolation and possible desperation. This context matters greatly because God often meets His people precisely in their moments of greatest need and fear.

God's Timing: The biblical text implies that this was a divinely appointed moment. Jacob could have stopped to rest anywhere, but he ended up in a specific place that, unbeknownst to him at the time, had profound spiritual significance. This was not an accident but part of God's providential design. In the same way, many significant encounters in Scripture occur at moments when people least expect them. For instance, Moses encountered God at the burning bush while tending sheep. Elijah heard God's still, small voice in the wilderness when he was running from Jezebel. God's timing underscores the message that He is sovereign and that revelations often come when we are most receptive or most in need.

The Purpose of the Encounter

Reaffirming the Covenant: The core purpose of this dream was to reaffirm the covenant promises made to Abraham and Isaac—now to be extended through Jacob. Despite Jacob's flawed character and questionable methods, God chose to appear to him, showing that the fulfillment of divine promises does not hinge on human merit but on God's grace and faithfulness. In Genesis 28:13–14, the Lord reiterates that Jacob's descendants will be numerous, that they will inherit the land, and that through them all nations of the earth will be blessed.

This reaffirmation signals that God's grand redemptive plan continues, even amid human failure. Through Abraham, Isaac, and now Jacob, God would form a covenant people who would eventually become the nation of Israel, from which the Messiah would come. Thus, the dream was not just a personal comfort for Jacob; it also served a historical and theological purpose in the greater biblical narrative.

Personal Reassurance: At a more immediate level, God addresses Jacob's personal fears. Jacob may well have wondered if the blessing he received through deceit would stand, or if God disapproved of his actions. Yet God does not appear in the dream with anger or condemnation; instead, He assures Jacob, saying, "I am with you and will keep you wherever you go" (Genesis 28:15). Such words would have brought immense comfort to a man who was literally fleeing for his life, unsure if he would ever return home.

By affirming that "I will not leave you until I have done what I have promised you," God demonstrates His unchanging nature. This moment also functions as an extension of divine mercy to Jacob. While Jacob's actions were certainly flawed, God chose to operate within the framework of His sovereign plan, continuing to shape Jacob's character through various trials and blessings.

The Message of the Encounter

Heaven's Accessibility: One of the most striking images in the dream is that of a ladder or stairway connecting heaven and earth, with angels ascending and descending on it. This conveys the message that heaven is not distant or disengaged from earthly affairs. Rather, there is an open channel through which God's angels carry out divine directives. This imagery, which becomes the impetus for later theological reflections, signifies that God is intimately involved in the world's happenings, particularly the lives of His chosen.

For Jacob, the vision underscores that he is not alone. Even if he cannot see God's presence in his everyday reality, the ladder image reveals constant heavenly activity, suggesting that there is more going on than meets the eye. Angels, as God's messengers and servants, are shown actively moving between heaven and earth, symbolizing care, protection, and guidance.

God's Sovereignty and Grace: Another key aspect of the message is the emphasis on divine sovereignty. Jacob did not orchestrate this dream; God took the initiative. By revealing Himself and reaffirming the covenant, God shows that His plans will unfold, often in unexpected ways and through imperfect individuals. This demonstrates that the ultimate success of the covenant does not rest on human righteousness but on God's unwavering faithfulness.

The dream also highlights grace. Despite Jacob's history of deceit, God does not revoke His blessing. This underscores the biblical theme that God's gifts are irrevocable (Romans 11:29) and that His dealings with humanity are often marked by unconditional favor. Jacob is neither the first nor the last recipient of divine blessings despite moral failings; rather, he becomes a testament to how God can transform and use imperfect people to accomplish His purposes.

The Vision of the Ladder

Symbolism and Meaning: The ladder or stairway is central to the dream's imagery. While some translations call it a "ladder," others describe it as a "stairway" or "ramp." Regardless of the exact architectural detail, the function is the same: it provides a point of contact between heaven and earth. The angels' movement indicates a two-way interaction: from God to humanity and from humanity back to God, facilitated by divine initiative.

Future Implications: The ladder is a foreshadowing of Jesus Christ (see John 1:51), the ultimate link between heaven and earth. This sets the stage for the fuller revelation in the New Testament, where Jesus Himself references Jacob's dream, suggesting that He is the true access point to the Father. Thus, while the immediate purpose was to comfort Jacob and reaffirm the covenant, the vision of the ladder resonates throughout redemptive history, culminating in the person and work of Christ.

Spiritual Awakening: Upon waking, Jacob declares, "Surely the Lord is in this place, and I did not know it" (Genesis 28:16). This statement reflects a sudden shift in Jacob's awareness. He realizes that the mundane location where he lay his head on a stone was actually charged with divine presence. This awakening to the reality of God's nearness underscores how often we may go about our lives oblivious to the presence of God. The vision thus serves as a catalyst for Jacob to acknowledge and revere the God who is intimately present, even in seemingly ordinary or lonely circumstances.

For those who read this message today, the dream at Bethel speaks to how God can break into our journeys—often at unexpected places and times—opening our eyes to His plan and presence. Even in our darkest nights or loneliest journeys, God has a way of revealing Himself, assuring us that His purposes stand firm and that His watchful care extends wherever we may go.

2.2. The Significance in Jacob's Life

Jacob's dream at Bethel was more than a fleeting spiritual experience. It would transform and define him for the rest of his life. Though Jacob was already the bearer of the patriarchal blessing, he lacked personal conviction and a deep relationship with God. The dream ushered in a new phase of spiritual awareness, one that would shape his identity and his relationship with the Lord. In this section, we will explore the spiritual significance of the dream and Jacob's immediate and long-term responses to what he saw and heard.

Spiritual Significance: An Encounter That Marks a Life

From Fear to Faith: Before the dream, Jacob was primarily driven by fear—fear of Esau, fear of the unknown, and perhaps fear of the consequences of his deceit. The dream at Bethel confronted him with the reality of God's presence and plan. The immediate effect upon awakening was a sense of awe and reverence. Genesis 28:17 records his response: "How awesome is this place! This is none other than the house of God, and this is the gate of heaven." The awareness that he had encountered something profoundly holy replaced his fear of Esau with the "fear of the Lord," which is the beginning of wisdom (Proverbs 9:10). Though Jacob would continue to struggle in various ways, this reverential fear became a new anchor in his life.

A Sense of Belonging: Jacob had left home uncertain about his standing—would he ever see his father again? Would Esau's anger subside? Where did he truly belong? Through the dream, God gave Jacob both a promise of land and a promise of continued presence: "I am with you and will keep you wherever you go..." (Genesis 28:15). This affirmation provided a spiritual and emotional anchor. Jacob now knew he belonged to God's covenant community, not by chance or by mere human arrangement, but by divine choice and appointment.

Revelation of God's Character: This encounter also imparted deeper revelation about who God is. Jacob learned that God is faithful and sovereign, overseeing the covenant from generation to generation. He also learned that God is personal and merciful, willing to engage with him despite his history of deceit. The dream shattered any notion of a distant deity: God was so near that Jacob exclaimed that the place itself was "the house of God." This revelation of divine closeness influenced Jacob's future prayers and actions, as he increasingly understood God to be a loving guardian, not an impersonal force.

Catalyst for Ongoing Transformation: Though the dream did not instantly transform Jacob's character, it was a catalyst for the journey of faith that would follow. In subsequent chapters, Jacob encounters various trials, including deception at the hands of his uncle Laban, conflict within his family, and the famous wrestling match with the "man" at Peniel (Genesis 32). Each of these can be traced back to seeds planted at Bethel, where

Jacob first recognized the active presence of the God of his fathers in his own life. Spiritual encounters often work this way: they begin a process of transformation that unfolds over time through obedience, perseverance, and further divine guidance.

Jacob's Response to the Dream

Erecting a Memorial: Upon waking, Jacob took the stone he had used as a pillow and set it up as a pillar, pouring oil on top of it (Genesis 28:18). This act was symbolic: it marked the spot as holy, commemorating the divine visitation. In the ancient Near East, the setting up of a pillar and the pouring of oil were acts of consecration, dedicating a place to a deity. This memorial would later serve as a physical reminder of the covenant and the encounter. For Jacob, it represented a new beginning, a tangible statement of faith in the God who appeared to him.

Naming the Place "Bethel": Jacob then named the place "Bethel," meaning "House of God." Previously, it had been called Luz. The renaming signified a new spiritual reality. Jacob was essentially testifying that what was once an ordinary location—an obscure city known as Luz—had become a sacred meeting point with the Almighty. The name change indicated Jacob's recognition of God's ownership and presence over that place. Throughout the Bible, naming or renaming often carries deep significance (e.g., Abram to Abraham, Sarai to Sarah, etc.), signaling transformation or divine purpose.

The place Jacob named "Bethel" is today identified as the modern-day village of Beitín in the West Bank, located a few kilometers northeast of Ramallah

Vow to Serve God: Perhaps the most significant response was Jacob's vow (Genesis 28:20–22). Jacob said, "If God will be with me and will keep me in this way that I go, and will give me bread to eat and clothing to wear... then the Lord shall be my God." At first glance, this can appear transactional, almost as if Jacob were bargaining with God. However, in the context of ancient Near Eastern culture, vows were common expressions of devotion and dependence. Jacob was not trying to manipulate God; he was expressing that he recognized God's lordship, but he also acknowledged his need for divine provision. This vow set in motion the official acceptance of the God of Abraham and Isaac as his own God.

Commitment of Tithing: Jacob added another detail: "Of all that you give me I will give a full tenth to you" (Genesis 28:22). This anticipates the concept of the tithe, a sacred offering to God that later became a formal part of Israel's worship system (Leviticus 27:30–32; Deuteronomy 14:22–29). Jacob's vow to tithe indicates his willingness to honor God materially, acknowledging that everything he receives ultimately comes from the Lord. It also underscores a heart of gratitude and dependence on God. Though this vow would be tested over the course of his life, it was a foundational step toward cultivating a habit of giving back to God in recognition of His blessings.

Lessons from Jacob's Response

Worship in Response to God's Revelation: One of the most important takeaways from Jacob's reaction is his immediate act of worship—setting up the pillar, naming the place Bethel, and vowing to serve God. When God reveals Himself, the proper response is reverential worship and the dedication of one's life to Him.

Memorializing God's Work: Jacob's pillar and naming of Bethel highlight the importance of remembering what God has done. In today's context, believers might keep journals, partake in Communion, or celebrate personal milestones to remember God's faithfulness and presence.

Making Vows or Commitments Carefully: Jacob's vow demonstrates that spiritual commitments are a normal part of a living relationship with God, but they must be approached reverently and responsibly. Instead of bargaining with God, believers can follow Jacob's lead by acknowledging dependence on God's provision and pledging loyalty.

Continuing Journey Toward Maturity: Bethel was a starting point, not a final destination. Jacob still had to mature spiritually, facing many challenges that tested his character. Likewise, an initial spiritual encounter with God is only the beginning of a life-long journey of faith, obedience, and transformation.

Finding Our Own Bethel: Modern Christians may find themselves in crisis moments or seasons of loneliness, much like Jacob. Recognizing that God can and often does reveal Himself in those moments invites us to look for a "Bethel" experience, a place or a moment where God's presence becomes undeniably real and catalytic for our growth.

Significance for Jacob and for Us

For Jacob, the Bethel dream became the foundation of his personal faith journey—a transition from second-hand faith inherited from his father to a direct relationship with God. The significance was monumental: it gave him a new identity, a renewed vision for his future, and a sense of security in God's covenant promises.

Spiritual Encounters in the Christian Life: In the Christian tradition, moments reminiscent of Bethel may come through various means: the reading of Scripture, a powerful sermon, a personal revelation, or a profound sense of God's presence during prayer. While not all believers will see a ladder extending into heaven, many can testify to specific times when God's reality broke through in a transformative way. Such experiences often mark a turning point or serve as a strong confirmation of God's call or promise.

Engaging with God's Covenant Promises: Like Jacob, Christians are heirs of a promise—this time, the new covenant sealed by the blood of Christ (Matthew 26:28; Hebrews 9:15). The dream at Bethel foreshadows the greater revelation of God's faithfulness in Christ, reminding us that our salvation and our sanctification rest on God's unchanging promise, not on our perfection. This should encourage believers to persevere, to lean into God's grace, and to remember that even when we are unfaithful, God remains faithful (2 Timothy 2:13).

Living in Awe of God's Nearness: Jacob's exclamation—"Surely the Lord is in this place, and I did not know it"—points to a deep spiritual truth: God's presence often precedes our awareness. The significance of Bethel is that it awakened Jacob to the reality that God was intimately involved in his journey all along. For Christians, the Holy Spirit's indwelling presence (1 Corinthians 6:19–20) signifies that we carry Bethel with us wherever we go. Every place can become a "house of God" if we cultivate awareness of His presence.

2.3. Who Was That Revealed to Jacob?

In Genesis 28:12, the text describes angels of God ascending and descending on the ladder. Shortly thereafter, in verse 13, it states, "And behold, the Lord stood above it..." The interplay between angels and the Lord in this passage, and indeed throughout the Old Testament, often raises questions about the nature of these angelic appearances and whether some of them might be direct manifestations of God Himself.

Understanding Angels in the Old Testament

Messengers of God: The Hebrew word for angel, *mal'ak*, generally means "messenger." These beings are portrayed as God's servants, carrying out His will. In the Old Testament, angels appear to deliver messages (e.g., Gabriel to Daniel), protect God's people (as in the case of Elisha and his servant seeing the angelic army in 2 Kings 6), and even execute judgment (e.g., the angel of the Lord striking down the Assyrians in 2 Kings 19:35). In Genesis 28, the angels ascending and descending the ladder reflect constant communication between heaven and earth, indicating that God's providential care and sovereign rule are operative in Jacob's life.

Various Angelic Encounters: Jacob's dream is not an isolated example of angelic activity in the patriarchal narratives. Angels also appear to Abraham (Genesis 18), to Hagar (Genesis 16 and 21), and later again to Jacob (Genesis 32:1–2) where Jacob exclaims, "This is God's camp!" The repeated angelic manifestations underline God's personal involvement in guiding and protecting the patriarchs. However, the text in Genesis 28:13 specifically says that "the Lord stood above it," moving from a general mention of angels to a direct mention of God's presence.

The Complexity of "The Angel of the Lord"

A Special Title: In several Old Testament passages, there appears a figure called "the Angel of the Lord" (in Hebrew, *mal'ak YHWH*). This being often speaks as God, receives worship, and wields divine authority (e.g., Exodus 3:2–6, Judges 6:11–24). The text sometimes shifts fluidly between calling this figure "the angel of the Lord" and simply "the Lord." This phenomenon suggests that this figure is more than a regular angelic messenger. Some theologians interpret these appearances as *theophanies*—visible manifestations of God Himself, while others see them as Christophanies—pre-incarnate appearances of the Second Person of the Trinity, Jesus.

The Angel of the Lord and Jacob: When we ask, "Who was the angel that revealed to Jacob?" we confront the possibility that the "angel" could be the very presence of God in a tangible or visible form, especially given that the text quickly moves to saying, "the Lord stood above it." While Genesis 28 does not explicitly label this figure "the Angel of the Lord," there is a strong biblical pattern of God revealing Himself through a mediating figure that is both distinct from and yet identified with God.

Later in Jacob's life, we see a similar pattern in Genesis 32, where Jacob wrestles with "a man" until daybreak. By the end of the encounter, Jacob concludes, "I have seen God face to face, and yet my life has been delivered" (Genesis 32:30). This passage, often interpreted as a theophany or a Christophany, parallels the complexity of angelic or divine appearances in the Old Testament. Hence, the identity of the angel in Genesis 28 may also be closely aligned with a direct manifestation of God.

God Himself: Why Appear in This Manner?

The condescension to Human Capacity: One reason God might choose to appear through an angelic or anthropomorphic figure is to accommodate human limitations. As Exodus 33:20 states, "You cannot see my face, for man shall not see me and live." The fullness of God's glory is beyond human comprehension, so God often veils His presence in order to communicate with humanity. Whether through a burning bush, a pillar of cloud and fire, or an angelic being, these manifestations ensure that God can reveal Himself without overwhelming or destroying finite creatures.

Progressive Revelation: Throughout the Old Testament, there is a progression in how God discloses Himself. These theophanies lay the groundwork for the eventual full revelation in Jesus Christ, who is described as "the radiance of the glory of God and the exact imprint of his nature" (Hebrews 1:3). In Genesis 28, God's appearance above the ladder can be seen as part of this unfolding revelation: God graciously shows Jacob that He is not a distant deity but is intimately involved in human affairs, bridging heaven and earth. This sets the stage for understanding Jesus as the ultimate "Ladder" or mediator between God and humanity (John 1:51).

Affirming the Covenant: Another reason for this direct or near-direct appearance of God is to affirm the weight and importance of the covenant promises. By showing Himself to Jacob, God validates the same promise given to Abraham and Isaac, thus cementing Jacob's role in salvation history. An ordinary angel might deliver a message, but when the biblical text transitions to "the Lord" speaking, it underscores that God Himself is establishing or reaffirming His covenant with Jacob. This direct involvement assures Jacob of the certainty and gravity of the promises.

Scriptural Pointers for Divine Presence in Genesis 28

Shifting Language: The text starts with angels ascending and descending (v. 12) and quickly notes, "Behold, the Lord stood above it" (v. 13). The shift from plural angels to singular "the Lord" signifies a move from a scene of God's servants to God Himself.

First-Person Divine Speech: In verses 13–15, the speaker uses the first person ("I am the Lord," "I will give," "I will not leave you"). In the Old Testament, angels typically introduce themselves as messengers speaking on God's behalf (e.g., "Thus says the Lord..."), but here the speech is direct as if from God Himself.

Repetition of Covenant Language: The blessings stated—descendants, land, and global blessing—are the heart of the Abrahamic covenant. These promises originate from God alone, reinforcing that the speaker is indeed the Lord.

Jacob's Reaction: Jacob exclaims, "Surely the Lord is in this place," NOT "Surely an angel is in this place" (Genesis 28:16). This suggests that Jacob perceived the presence of God directly. He names the place "Bethel," the house of God, not "the house of God's angel."

Why This Matters for Believers Today

God's Initiative in Revelation: The discussion about the angelic identity highlights that God always takes the first step in revealing Himself. Just as Jacob did not conjure or summon angels but simply received the vision, believers must remember that salvation and revelation are acts of divine grace. We do not climb to God by our own efforts; God descends to us, meeting us in our condition of need.

Divine Presence in Ordinary Places: Jacob's experience teaches that what seems like an ordinary or even a forlorn location can become a holy place when God reveals Himself. For modern believers, this underscores that no place is too mundane or too distant for God's intervention. The question "Who was the angel?" becomes secondary to the overarching truth that God is present, offering guidance, comfort, and covenantal promises.

Bridging Heaven and Earth: If, as many Christians believe, the ultimate meaning of Jacob's ladder points to Jesus Christ, then the angelic presence in Genesis 28 prefigures the new and living way (Hebrews 10:20) Jesus opened for believers. The question of the angel's identity connects to the broader biblical theme of God bridging the gap between the heavenly and the earthly realms. In Jesus, the perfect mediator, we see the fullest and most personal expression of this divine condescension and revelation.

2.4. The Personal Application for Today's Christians

The Dream at Bethel is an ancient event, set in a time and culture far removed from the modern world. Yet, Scripture's enduring power lies in its ability to speak across millennia, guiding believers in every age. Jacob's encounter with God—marked by angels, a ladder, and divine promises—contains timeless principles that can deeply influence the faith and practice of today's Christians.

Recognizing God's Presence in Unexpected Places

Jacob's Surprise: Jacob did not expect to meet God on the road to Haran. Fleeing from family turmoil, he chose a random place to rest. Upon waking, he exclaimed, "Surely the Lord is in this place, and I did not know it." For contemporary believers, this highlights that God's presence can manifest in the most ordinary or even dire circumstances. Whether we find ourselves in a hospital room, a workplace, or the loneliness of a long drive, God is able to make His presence known.

Cultivating Awareness: One practical way to apply this truth is to foster a habit of spiritual mindfulness. Before beginning the day or undertaking any major task, Christians can pray for God to open their eyes to His presence. This conscious invitation helps shift our perspective from seeing the world as purely secular to recognizing the sacred dimension in all aspects of life. Journaling daily experiences of perceived divine intervention or guidance can further deepen this awareness.

Trusting in God's Sovereign Plan

Reassurance in the Covenant: In Genesis 28:15, God told Jacob, "I am with you and will keep you wherever you go... I will not leave you until I have done what I have promised you." This promise, while specific to Jacob and the Abrahamic covenant, reflects God's unchanging nature. For Christians, God has made an even better covenant through Christ, assuring believers, "I will never leave you nor forsake you" (Hebrews 13:5).

Overcoming Anxiety and Fear: In a world filled with uncertainty—political upheaval, economic instability, personal trials—the promise of God's abiding presence is a source of peace. When anxious thoughts arise, Christians can draw strength from knowing that God's purposes transcend current circumstances. Engaging in scriptural meditation on verses like Romans 8:28 ("And we know that for those who love God all things work together for good...") or Philippians 4:6–7 ("Do not be anxious about anything...") reiterates that God's sovereignty is our assurance.

Patience in God's Timing: Jacob did not see the immediate fulfillment of all God's promises; he faced years of struggle and labor under Laban. Similarly, believers might wait for healing, breakthroughs, or the restoration of relationships. The Bethel encounter teaches that while God's promises are sure, their fulfillment often unfolds over time. Embracing patience and steadfast faith becomes easier when we anchor ourselves in God's character rather than our fleeting emotions.

Entering into Personal Covenant with God

Jacob's Vow: Jacob made a vow: if God provided for his needs and protected him, then "the Lord shall be my God" (Genesis 28:20–21). While modern believers operate under the grace of the new covenant, there is still value in making personal commitments to the Lord. A vow can be a way of aligning our priorities with God's purposes, as long as it is motivated by faith and not by an attempt to bargain with God.

Developing a Rule of Life: A contemporary application might be creating a "rule of life," a structured set of spiritual disciplines and commitments that reflect a personal dedication to God. This could include: Regular times of prayer and Bible study, Commitment to tithe or practice generous giving, Active involvement in a local church community, Service to the marginalized or missions work, and Engaging in personal evangelization.

Such commitments, done in response to God's faithfulness, become practical frameworks that shape our daily walk with Christ.

Embracing the True Ladder: Jesus Christ

Personal Relationship with Christ: Jacob's ladder finds its ultimate fulfillment in Jesus, who grants believers direct access to God. Reflecting on Jacob's dream can rekindle appreciation for the depth of salvation in Christ. Christians can cultivate intimacy with Jesus through daily devotion, acknowledging Him as the only bridge between them and the Father.

Confidence in Prayer and Worship: Knowing that Jesus is our mediator encourages a bold approach to prayer. We do not need to climb a literal ladder to reach God; Jesus has already spanned that distance. This truth can transform worship from a ritual to a heartfelt response of gratitude and awe.

Hope in Eternal Realities: Jacob's dream underscores a heavenly reality intersecting with the earthly realm. For Christians, this reality is epitomized in the promise of eternal life with God. Remembering that our citizenship is in heaven (Philippians 3:20) can inspire greater holiness, generosity, and passion for the gospel.

Ministering Under Angelic Oversight

Angels Ascending and Descending: The angels in Jacob's dream were ascending and descending to carry out God's will. Similarly, Hebrews 1:14 suggests that angels are "ministering spirits" sent to serve those who inherit salvation. This knowledge provides comfort: believers do not undertake their spiritual journey alone; the heavenly hosts work invisibly to aid them in accomplishing God's purposes.

Practical Mission Engagement: While the supernatural realm remains largely unseen, believers can still cooperate with God's work by being sensitive to the Holy Spirit's leading. Whether sharing the gospel, volunteering in community outreach, or simply offering kindness to a neighbor, Christians participate in the divine mission. The ladder imagery reminds us that our earthly actions are connected to heaven's priorities.

Taking Steps of Faith

From Bethel to the Unknown: Jacob did not remain at Bethel; he proceeded on his journey, carrying with him the promise of God's presence. Modern Christians can similarly use spiritual encounters as launchpads for obedience. When God speaks or confirms a calling, the next step is action—whether it's reconciling a relationship, pursuing a particular ministry, or changing career paths for a kingdom purpose.

Risk and Adventure: Faith is inherently risky; it involves stepping into the unknown with trust in God's Word. The memory of previous "Bethel" moments—where God confirmed His guidance—can fuel courage. Just as Jacob embarked on a difficult journey, believers today can face challenges knowing that the God of Bethel goes before them.

Sharing the Bethel Experience with Others

A Light to the Nations: God's promise to bless all nations through Abraham's descendants (Genesis 12:3) echoes in Jacob's dream. For Christians, the Great Commission (Matthew 28:18–20) is a continuation of this mandate. Just as Jacob eventually became Israel, forming the foundation of God's covenant people, the Church is called to be a light to the world, extending the blessings of Christ to every nation.

Testimony as Evangelism: Personal stories of encountering God—modern Bethel moments—can be powerful tools of evangelism. When believers share how God met them in their need, provided direction, or answered prayers, they offer tangible evidence of God's reality. This personal testimony can open hearts to the gospel more effectively than abstract arguments.

Living in Hope and Expectation

Jacob's Long Journey: Jacob's journey did not end at Bethel; he would have other encounters (including wrestling with God at Peniel) and would face family struggles. Still, the initial dream gave him an enduring hope. In the same way, Christians navigate life's ups and downs under the umbrella of God's promises.

Looking Forward: The Bethel dream was but a prelude to Jacob's eventual return and the broader narrative of Israel's birth. Today, believers look forward to Christ's return and the consummation of God's kingdom. Each worship experience, each answered prayer, and each moment of divine revelation foreshadows the day when heaven and earth will be fully united (Revelation 21:1–3). This eschatological hope inspires perseverance, encouraging Christians to remain faithful through trials and to continue spreading the gospel until Jesus comes.

Jacob's dream at Bethel, though an ancient event, speaks to modern believers about God's faithfulness, His desire to reveal Himself, and the transforming power of personal encounters with the Divine. The lessons are manifold:

1. **God's Presence**: Always closer than we think, ready to meet us in the ordinary.

2. **Worship and Remembrance**: Essential responses to God's revelation, grounding our faith in tangible memorials.

3. **Faith and Covenant**: A call to trust God's promises, make personal commitments, and walk obediently in His will.

4. **Christ-Centered Reality**: Recognizing Jesus as the ultimate ladder that unites heaven and earth, granting believers constant access to God's throne of grace.

5. **Mission and Testimony**: Extending God's blessing to others, serving as a witness to His redemptive work.

By applying these insights, Christians can transform everyday life into a continual journey with God—much like Jacob, who left Bethel forever changed. Even if we do not see a physical ladder with angels ascending and descending, we live with the assurance that in Christ, heaven is open, and God is actively working in and through us. May we, like Jacob, arise each day, consecrate our ordinary "stones," and proclaim with reverent awe: "Surely the Lord is in this place!"

If you found this message encouraging, please share it with others who may benefit. God Bless.

3. Second Encounter – The Dream at Haran

Angel of God instructed him to leave Laban's house.

Genesis 31:10-13 describes another pivotal moment in Jacob's life when God speaks to him in a dream during his time in Haran, serving his uncle Laban. This is recognized as Jacob's second major encounter with God, following his first well-known dream at Bethel. At Bethel, Jacob saw a ladder (or stairway) connecting heaven and earth, and God reaffirmed the covenant promises first given to Abraham and Isaac. Now, years have passed, and Jacob has endured complex family relationships, especially with Laban. He has married Leah and Rachel, fathered children, and worked tirelessly for two decades. During that time, Laban repeatedly changed his wages and tested Jacob's resolve.

In this second encounter, Jacob dreams about male goats that are streaked, speckled, and spotted, and the angel of God then speaks to him. The purpose of this encounter goes beyond mere symbolism of livestock multiplication; it reveals God's continued presence, His careful oversight of Jacob's life, and His desire to lead Jacob toward his true home.

3.1. Purpose of Second Encounter?

After escaping from his brother Esau's wrath, Jacob found refuge with his maternal uncle, Laban. There, he agreed to work for seven years to marry Rachel, only to be deceived into marrying Leah first. Another seven years ensued, allowing Jacob to finally marry Rachel, and then he continued to work for Laban, caring for large flocks and herds. Over time, Jacob's labor was richly blessed by God, resulting in the birth of many children and the accumulation of wealth. However, it wasn't straightforward prosperity: Laban continually sought to control the situation, changing Jacob's wages multiple times (Genesis 31:7).

At this juncture, Jacob experiences frustration, exhaustion, and suspicion, wondering if he is ever going to be truly free from Laban's manipulations. It is precisely into this context that God speaks through a dream—an assurance that Jacob's growth in wealth and flocks is not merely random fortune but a direct result of God's intervention. The dream underscores a more significant point: the same God who met Jacob at Bethel has never left his side.

Reaffirmation of the Covenant and Direction: One central purpose of this dream is to remind Jacob of the covenant promises. At Bethel, God told Jacob, "I am the Lord, the God of your father Abraham and the God of Isaac", and He promised Jacob numerous descendants, land, and divine blessing. By the time we reach Genesis 31, Jacob has indeed become the father of many children, yet he is still in a foreign land, under the sway of a difficult in-law. The dream at Haran therefore reaffirms that God's plan is still on track. Although years have passed, and circumstances have changed, God's faithfulness has not diminished.

Moreover, this second divine encounter has a practical dimension: God instructs Jacob to leave Haran and return to the land of his fathers. He says, "Now arise, get out of this land, and return to the land of your family" (Genesis 31:13). This directive is essential for Jacob's next steps in fulfilling his destiny as the heir of Abraham's and Isaac's blessing. The dream's purpose is to propel Jacob forward into obedience, calling him to trust God enough to leave behind the relative familiarity of Haran—even with its challenges—and journey back to Canaan, the land of promise.

The Message of Divine Oversight and Justice: Another dimension to the purpose of this encounter is to reveal that God sees and intervenes on behalf of the oppressed. Jacob confesses to Rachel and Leah: "Your father has deceived me and changed my wages ten times, but God did not allow him to hurt me" (Genesis 31:7). This statement resonates with a broader biblical theme: God is the defender of those who are mistreated, whether it is Hagar in the wilderness or the Israelites under Egyptian bondage. Jacob's dream provides a clear message that the blessings he experiences—specifically, the unusually patterned goats and sheep that multiply under his care—are the result of God's intervention. God ensures that Jacob's compensation is commensurate with the hard work and injustice he has endured.

This message conveys that God is not indifferent to Jacob's struggles. Each time Laban changes the conditions, God changes the breeding patterns so that Jacob prospers. Such a miraculous outcome defies natural explanation. Hence, the angel in Jacob's dream reminds him that God is the architect of this blessing. The deeper point is that, even when humans manipulate or exploit a situation, God remains sovereign and can turn all circumstances for His divine purpose.

The Vision Itself: God's Faithfulness on Display: In the dream, Jacob sees male goats that are streaked, speckled, or spotted mating with the flocks. This vision is specific to Jacob's situation: he had arranged with Laban that any streaked or spotted livestock would belong to Jacob. The dream directly ties Jacob's wealth to God's action. It is a vivid demonstration of how God orchestrates even the mundane details of life—down to breeding patterns—to fulfill His promises.

Vision Confirming God's Character and Sovereignty: The dream also reaffirms who God is: the "God of Bethel" who heard Jacob's vow, accepted his worship, and established a covenant. The phrase "I am the God of Bethel" is deeply significant. It reminds Jacob that God is not just a far-off deity but the same personal Lord who revealed Himself years prior. For Jacob, this continuity of identity underscores a core truth about God: He is unchanging, consistent, and reliable.

Equally important is the demonstration of God's sovereignty. Despite Laban's manipulations, it is God who controls fertility, prosperity, and the outcome of every situation. The dream reveals that Jacob's flourishing is not purely a result of his own cunning (although Jacob does act shrewdly in the breeding process); behind any human strategy lies God's ultimate will. This reminder of divine sovereignty is a lesson about humility: even when Jacob tries to manage the situation, the final credit belongs to God.

This has a resonant message for believers today: No matter how complicated or unjust our circumstances, we serve a God who sees, cares, and intervenes. He remains faithful to His promises, guides us through seasons of turmoil, and ultimately leads us home—physically, spiritually, and eternally. The vision stands as a testament that God does not abandon His people in the midst of trials. When God calls us forward, He provides not only instruction but also assurance of His presence, reminding us that our journeys, like Jacob's, are under divine orchestration and grace.

3.2. Spiritual Significance in Jacob's Life

A Catalyst for Transformation: Jacob's life story can be summarized as a process of transformation, guided by divine encounters and personal struggles. From the moment he tricked his brother Esau out of the birthright and the paternal blessing, Jacob carried with him the reputation of a cunning schemer. This second encounter with God in Haran is significant precisely because it underscores a shift in Jacob's understanding of God, and the covenant. While Jacob's first dream at

Bethel was more of a wake-up call—God making an initial statement of presence—this second dream catalyzes a more thorough transformation in Jacob's character.

In spiritual terms, the encounter highlights that sanctification often comes through a series of revelations and trials. Over the course of twenty years, Jacob has dealt with the consequences of deception, faced deception himself at Laban's hands, and learned that God's blessing is not something to be seized by human craftiness but is instead a divine gift. This second dream affirms that Jacob's success in breeding livestock is ultimately orchestrated by God, not by his own cunning.

Affirming Divine Calling and Identity: The significance of this dream also includes its role in reaffirming Jacob's identity as the heir of the Abrahamic covenant. Recall that at Bethel, God promised that Jacob's descendants would be as numerous as the dust of the earth and that all nations would be blessed through him. Over time, Jacob might have questioned how these promises would come to pass. He was an exile in Haran, effectively working as a servant to Laban. Perhaps he wondered if he could ever return to Canaan without facing retribution from Esau.

The second encounter clarifies that God has not forsaken His plan. In the dream, the Angel of Lord identifies Himself with the God of Bethel, a deliberate reminder of the initial promise. This continuity is crucial for Jacob's sense of calling. It shows that even in what may appear to be a detour from the promised land, God remains intimately involved in Jacob's trajectory. For Jacob, this encounter must have been a profound reassurance that his identity was not merely that of a fugitive or a son-in-law caught in a complicated household; he was, in fact, the bearer of an eternal covenant.

God's Presence in the Midst of Trials: Spiritually, the dream highlights the truth that God's presence is not restricted to holy sites or special seasons of life. Previously, Jacob had encountered God in the dramatic setting of

Bethel, which he recognized as "the house of God" and "the gate of heaven" (Genesis 28:17). One might mistakenly think that such powerful revelations only occur in sacred spaces. Yet here, God meets Jacob again in Haran, amid the ordinary realities of daily life: conflict over wages, caring for flocks, raising children, and trying to navigate a difficult family relationship.

For Jacob, the significance is profound: God's watchful eye and guiding hand are available not just in obviously sacred moments but in the mundane. This recognition should not be understated. In many ways, it is easier to believe that God is near when we are in a spiritual high point, perhaps at a place like Bethel. But the message of this dream is that God can show up anytime and anywhere to speak, direct, and bless His people.

Jacob's Response: Obedience Mixed With Hesitation: Jacob's immediate response to the dream is recorded in Genesis 31:14-16, where he shares the vision with Rachel and Leah. He explains how God has blessed him in spite of Laban's repeated attempts to cheat him and how God has now commanded him to return to his homeland. Rachel and Leah, recognizing that their father has largely alienated them and treated them as outsiders, agree with Jacob's plan. Their support is critical; if Jacob's wives had refused, the journey could have been even more complicated.

Jacob's obedience is noteworthy. While his personality may still exhibit shades of hesitation or fear—he ultimately leaves surreptitiously, without informing Laban—he does, nonetheless, act on the divine command. His initial departure from Laban is done quietly, suggesting that he is both determined to obey God yet also aware of Laban's potential fury. This mixture of faith and caution exemplifies how biblical characters often step out in obedience despite lingering uncertainties.

A Deeper Dependence on God: Part of the spiritual significance of this encounter is that it pushes Jacob toward deeper reliance on God. After the dream, Jacob is forced to trust that returning to Canaan will not lead to destruction at the hands of Esau or some other unforeseen danger. By leaving the comfort zone of Haran—where he had established a life, however challenging—Jacob is essentially placing his future in God's hands. This aligns closely with the call of faith that pervades Scripture, from Abraham's departure from Ur to the New Testament's exhortation for believers to "walk by faith, not by sight" (2 Corinthians 5:7).

The fact that Jacob chooses to pack up his entire household—wives, children, servants, and extensive flocks—and embark on a long journey reveals that he is learning to trust the God who spoke to him. Jacob's departure from Haran under God's directive marks the beginning of a new chapter in his life, one that will involve reconciliation with Esau, a renewed relationship with God, and eventually a renaming as "Israel."

Jacob's Gradual Growth in Faith: An important aspect of the spiritual significance is that Jacob's response is not perfect, yet it shows progress. He still resorts to stealth in his departure, indicating lingering fears. Nevertheless, Jacob clearly acknowledges that God has called him to leave. He no longer doubts God's ability to provide for him, since God has already proven that He can multiply livestock beyond natural expectation. Jacob's growth, therefore, is incremental yet evident.

This incremental growth mirrors the experience of many believers. We often vacillate between trust and doubt, boldness and fear, and yet God patiently leads us forward. The significance of Jacob's second dream is that it not only clarifies his external circumstances—how he will earn his wages, when and where to move—but it also functions as a spiritual milestone. From this point on, Jacob becomes increasingly aware of God's hand in his life.

3.3. Who Revealed to Jacob?

The "Angel of God": Genesis 31:11 records Jacob's words: "Then the angel of God said to me in the dream, 'Jacob.' And I said, 'Here I am.'" This figure, referred to as "the angel of God," is closely associated with the Lord Himself. The language used here—and in many Old Testament passages—suggests more than a mere heavenly messenger. In fact, biblical scholars often debate whether "the angel of the Lord" (or "the angel of God") is simply an angelic being or a theophany (a manifestation of God Himself).

In verse 13, the angel says, "I am the God of Bethel," which intensifies the debate. If this were simply a created angel, we would expect the angel to speak on behalf of God but not necessarily to identify as God. Yet in Genesis 31:13, the angel links Himself directly to the God who had appeared to Jacob at Bethel. This is strong evidence that the angel speaking to Jacob is a divine manifestation—often referred to as the "angel of Yahweh"—who can speak with the full authority and identity of God.

A Foreshadowing of the Incarnation: Some Christian theologians see these Old Testament appearances of the "angel of the Lord" as foreshadowings or previews of the incarnation of Jesus Christ. While the text of Genesis does not explicitly state this, later Christian reflection often interprets these manifestations as potential Christophanies—pre-incarnate appearances of the Second Person of the Trinity. While this interpretation is not unanimously held by all biblical scholars, it underscores a key point: the identity of the angel who speaks with God's own authority and claims to be God is a divine presence, not a mere created being.

In Genesis 31, if we accept that this angel is a theophany, then Jacob is essentially conversing directly with God in his dream. This lines up with the angel's statement in verse 13 that He is the very one who met Jacob at Bethel. There is no separate being introduced in the text; it is the same God who earlier promised to be with Jacob, who now reiterates that promise and instructs him to return home.

The Authority of the Angelic Messenger: When the angel says, "I have seen all that Laban has done to you" (Genesis 31:12), it emphasizes omniscience, a divine trait. No created angel claims personal oversight in such a direct, possessive sense. Typically, angels in Scripture give glory to God or refer to God's knowledge. The wording here, combined with "I am the God of Bethel," cements the notion that Jacob is encountering more than a delegated messenger.

This point is crucial for understanding why Jacob obeys so promptly. While Jacob is certainly aware of God's power, this direct reminder that the One who gave him the Bethel promise is still watching over him holds enormous weight. Hearing from the "angel" that He is indeed the same God fosters immediate conviction in Jacob's heart.

Ultimately, whether one interprets the "angel of God" as a high-ranking angelic being speaking on God's behalf or as a theophany/Christophany, the main takeaway is that Jacob is receiving a direct and authoritative word from the Lord. The text itself leans heavily toward the interpretation of a theophany because of the explicit identification "I am the God of Bethel." This is a profound statement about God's willingness to step into history, communicate His will, and guide the covenantal lineage.

Thus, in answering "Who revealed to Jacob?" we find that this encounter is no mere human-like figure reciting a divine script. Instead, it is the voice and presence of the covenant God Himself, reminding Jacob that He sees injustice, orchestrates provision, and commands obedience. The uniqueness of this revelation underscores the seriousness of God's command for Jacob to leave Haran and the certainty that God's promises are moving forward, no matter the opposition or complexity of human relationships.

For believers today, reflecting on this question heightens our awareness of God's accessibility and sovereignty. The God who appeared to Jacob is still the same God who speaks through Scripture and the Holy Spirit. We need not relegate God's direct involvement to ancient times, for He remains active and present, orchestrating events, guiding believers, and sometimes revealing Himself in powerful ways to accomplish His redemptive purposes.

3. 4. The Personal Application for Today's Christians

Trusting in God's Sovereignty Amid Life's Complexities: The story of Jacob's second encounter with God in Haran provides numerous insights for Christians living in the modern world. One of the most immediate applications is learning to trust in God's sovereignty when life becomes complicated. Jacob found himself in a tangled web of family obligations, manipulations, and uncertain prospects. For twenty years, he dealt with frustration and injustice at Laban's hands. Yet, unbeknownst to Jacob at times, God was actively managing every detail—from the birth of children to the multiplication of his livestock—to fulfill the promise first made at Bethel.

In our own lives, we often face complicated relationships, difficult workplaces, and seasons of waiting where we feel taken advantage of or overlooked. The lesson from Jacob's dream is that God sees everything. He is not blind to the injustices or the hidden manipulations we encounter. When we feel oppressed or uncertain, Jacob's experience encourages us to cling to the assurance that God's plan can triumph even under manipulative circumstances.

Recognizing God's Presence in the Ordinary: Another application is that God's presence is not restricted to "holy" moments or special spiritual events. Jacob initially encountered God in a dramatic vision at Bethel, which he designated as a sacred space. It would be easy to assume God only appears in overtly spiritual contexts. Yet Jacob's second dream occurs during his routine life as a shepherd in Haran—tending flocks, raising children, and dealing with an untrustworthy uncle.

46

For believers today, this is a powerful reminder that God speaks and guides in the midst of our daily tasks. Whether we are at an office job, in a classroom, caring for a family at home, or engaged in ministry, God can reveal His will at any time. We need to cultivate a posture of listening, being open to the Holy Spirit's prompting in the mundane moments of life. Sometimes, the very challenges we face in day-to-day living become the platform where God demonstrates His faithfulness, just as He did for Jacob.

Obedience and Faith Even When Fear Persists: Jacob's response to the dream underscores that obedience does not always mean the absence of fear. Jacob left Haran quickly, aware of the potential risks if Laban discovered his plan prematurely. Similarly, we may sense God calling us to take a step of faith—changing jobs, relocating, confronting an injustice, or starting a new ministry. Our obedience might be accompanied by trembling because the future remains uncertain.

Yet Jacob's story reassures us that faithful obedience is still possible in the face of anxiety. The key is to hold firmly to the Word of God. Jacob had clear instructions from the "angel of God," and despite his apprehensions, he acted. For believers, Scripture provides many clear directives—to love our neighbors, to seek justice, to spread the Gospel, to live in holiness— and when we perceive the Holy Spirit leading us in specific ways, we too can take steps of obedience, trusting that the One who calls us will sustain us.

Embracing God's Timeframe and Method: One might wonder why Jacob had to wait twenty years before God gave him the green light to depart from Laban. Could God not have acted sooner, sparing Jacob some of the heartache? The lesson here is that God's timing is perfect. Through those twenty years, Jacob's character was being shaped. He learned humility, patience, and a deeper reliance on God. When he finally did leave Haran, he departed with a large family, substantial flocks, and a clearer understanding of God's guidance.

In the Christian life, waiting often refines us. While we might desire instant solutions or immediate changes in our circumstances, God might be molding our hearts, preparing opportunities, or orchestrating events beyond our knowledge. The personal application is to remain faithful and attentive during seasons of waiting. Just as Jacob discovered, God's plan eventually becomes evident, and the waiting period is never wasted in God's economy.

Learning to Listen for God's Voice: Jacob's second dream raises a practical question: how do we recognize God's leading today? While dreams and visions are not the sole means of divine communication, Scripture and personal testimony confirm that God can still use them. More commonly, believers discern God's voice through Scripture, prayer, wise counsel, and the inner witness of the Holy Spirit. Regardless of the method, the principle remains: we must be prepared to hear from God and respond.

Jacob's posture in the dream is instructive—he listens and responds with an attitude akin to "Here I am." For Christians, cultivating a lifestyle of prayer, worship, and Scripture meditation positions our hearts to hear God more clearly. When we are sensitive to the Holy Spirit, we can perceive nudges and confirmations that align with Scripture and wise counsel.

Living in Covenant Consciousness: A final application pertains to living with a consciousness of God's covenant. Jacob's second encounter repeatedly underscores that he is part of a larger covenantal storyline. Likewise, believers today live under the new covenant in Christ—a covenant of grace, redemption, and the indwelling presence of the Holy Spirit. Our daily actions, decisions, and relationships should reflect the reality that we, too, are in covenant with God.

This includes recognizing that God is actively writing our stories in alignment with His redemptive plan. While we may not father entire nations as Jacob did, we are called to be ambassadors of the Gospel (2

Corinthians 5:20), reflecting Christ's character in the world. When we remember that we are part of a covenant with the living God, it transforms how we handle difficulties, how we trust in times of uncertainty, and how we demonstrate faith and love to those around us.

In essence, Jacob's second encounter at Haran speaks volumes to Christians today. We learn that God's sovereign plan persists despite long stretches of difficulty, that His presence permeates the everyday and not just the "holy" times, and that obedience can proceed even when uncertainty looms. The personal application encourages us to trust God's justice, wait for His timing, remain attentive to His voice, and live fully aware of our covenant relationship with Him.

Just as Jacob eventually left Haran with renewed faith, stepping forward into the next phase of God's plan, we too can step out in faith—whether that step involves leaving a toxic environment, reconciling with a family member, or venturing into a new mission—knowing that the God who met Jacob is the same God who meets us. In Christ, we have the fullness of God's covenant promises, and He calls us to walk in the assurance that He sees, guides, and provides.

If you found this message encouraging, please share it with others who may benefit. God Bless.

4. Third Encounter – In person at Peniel

Wrestling with God, receiving a new name (Israel)

When we arrive at Genesis 32, Jacob is on the cusp of a potentially lethal confrontation with his estranged brother Esau. He is deeply afraid, remembering the animosity he had earned. In this stressful moment, he sends messengers to Esau, prepares gifts to appease him, and divides his family into camps to minimize potential losses should Esau attack. That night, however, something greater than his fear of Esau occurs: he finds himself alone by the Jabbok River and engages in a mysterious wrestling match with a man he soon recognizes as divine. This event changes his life forever.

4.1. Purpose of This Encounter?

The immediate purpose of the encounter at Peniel goes beyond a mere test of physical strength or stubborn will. Instead, it serves as a critical pivot in Jacob's spiritual journey. Jacob has spent much of his life struggling—whether it be with his brother, his father, his uncle, or with his circumstances. Yet these earlier struggles, while intense, never fully addressed the deeper issues rooted in Jacob's heart, such as his self-reliance, fear, and manipulative tendencies.

At the Jabbok, Jacob faces a divine opponent who simultaneously thwarts Jacob's controlling tendencies and invites him to a moment of profound surrender. The text says: "Then Jacob was left alone; and a Man wrestled with him until the breaking of day" (Genesis 32:24 NKJV). The wrestling match is an outward manifestation of the internal struggle Jacob has faced for much of his life. It forces Jacob to grapple with his limitations and realize that he cannot rely solely on his own cunning or physical prowess.

From a broader biblical standpoint, the encounter underlines that God seeks to shape Jacob into the man He intended him to be. By physically wrestling with Jacob, God brings him to a place of brokenness—both literal (in the form of his hip being dislocated) and metaphorical, as Jacob's pride and self-reliance must yield to God's authority.

Jacob's Transition From Fear to Encounter: Leading up to the wrestling, Jacob is clearly terrified of Esau. He arranges elaborate strategies to protect his loved ones and secure favor. He even prays a heartfelt prayer (Genesis 32:9–12), appealing to God's past promises. Jacob's prayer is significant: though he is still scheming to control the future, he acknowledges that he owes everything to God's grace, remembering how he had crossed the Jordan with only a staff and now has two camps of people.

In this moment, the wrestling encounter seems to be God's sovereign method to force Jacob to place his absolute trust in the Almighty rather than in his own manipulations. By engaging him in a physical struggle, God effectively interrupts Jacob's anxious plans. This confrontation demands Jacob's immediate focus, and it compels him to consider where his true strength lies.

The Transformative Message of the Encounter: The name "Peniel" literally means "face of God," implying that Jacob came face-to-face with God in a deeply personal and life-altering way. This underscores the purpose of the encounter: Jacob's transformation from a man governed by fear and trickery into a man who relies on God and is given a new identity. When the stranger asks Jacob his name, it is not because He lacks information—God knows all things. Rather, it is an invitation for Jacob to confess who he has been: a "heel-grabber," a man defined by deceit. Only by acknowledging his identity can he be given a new one.

Hence, God changes Jacob's name to Israel, typically understood to mean "he struggles with God" or "God prevails." This renaming signals a radical shift. Israel will still face trials and conflicts, but he will do so under the promise and blessing of the One who overcame him in that wrestling match. From that night forward, Jacob limps—a physical testament to his encounter and a reminder that genuine spiritual blessings often come with a measure of pain and sacrifice.

The Broader Biblical Message and Redemptive History: At a theological level, God's willingness to "wrestle" with Jacob anticipates the incredible lengths to which He will go to fulfill His promises. Ultimately, this points to the incarnation of Jesus Christ, who literally stepped into human history and wrestled with sin and death on our behalf. The narrative of Jacob at Peniel is thus one thread in a grand tapestry of divine intervention and covenant faithfulness.

The purpose is not merely for Jacob's personal growth but to further God's unfolding plan. From this point forward, Jacob will move on—still flawed but forever changed. By extension, believers today can glean profound truths from this text: We all have areas where we wrestle with God, where our self-reliance collides with divine will. In those struggles, God desires to transform us, give us a new identity rooted in Christ, and remind us that true blessing is found in surrender rather than striving.

4.2. Spiritual Significance

The wrestling match at Peniel is more than just another milestone in Jacob's life; it is the hinge on which his story turns. Up to this moment, Jacob's narrative is characterized by recurring conflict—internal and external—most of which he attempts to manage or manipulate through his own ingenuity. Yet as the sun rises after his night-long struggle, Jacob emerges not as the same individual, but as someone marked by both blessing and a physical limp. This dual reality vividly illustrates that spiritual growth often comes through hardship, and true encounters with God rarely leave us unscathed or unchanged.

In the broader arc of Jacob's life, this is the definitive moment where his faith becomes deeply personal. Previously, Jacob often refers to God as the "God of my father Isaac" or the "God of Abraham" (Genesis 28:13). Yet after Peniel, his language shifts, and he begins to acknowledge God as his own. This progression signals a move from inherited religion to an experiential relationship, a pattern familiar in the lives of many believers today.

A Struggle for Surrender: Spiritually, the wrestling reveals the tension between human stubbornness and divine sovereignty. Throughout his life, Jacob strove to secure blessing on his own terms—whether it was through buying Esau's birthright for a bowl of stew or deceiving Isaac for the paternal blessing. However, at Peniel, Jacob can no longer rely on cunning. He is forced into a direct confrontation with One who far surpasses him in power, knowledge, and authority.

The night-long struggle culminates in Jacob's request: "I will not let you go unless you bless me" (Genesis 32:26). Initially, this may seem like an example of Jacob's tenacity bordering on audacity; yet within it is an admission of complete dependence. Jacob recognizes that blessing can no longer be taken by trickery or manipulation; it must be received from God Himself. This posture of clinging, even in pain, is central to the spiritual significance of the encounter: humility, persistence in seeking God, and the realization that apart from God's favor, all human efforts are futile.

Jacob's Response and Its Aftermath: In Genesis 32 Jacob acknowledge that he has seen God "face to face" (Genesis 32:30). In Hebrew narrative tradition, seeing God face-to-face was often considered lethal—no mortal can behold the fullness of God's glory and live (cf. Exodus 33:20). Yet Jacob survives, and the place receives the name Peniel (or Penuel), meaning "the face of God." This indicates that Jacob interprets the wrestling as a personal, theophanic encounter. His response is one of awe mixed with humility; he is aware that this was no ordinary opponent.

The Renaming: Jacob to Israel: A critical component of the passage is the renaming of Jacob to Israel (Genesis 32:28). Jacob's original name, tied to deception, pointed to his lifelong reliance on trickery. The new name, Israel, which is commonly interpreted as "he who struggles with God" or "God prevails," signifies an entirely new orientation.

This shift is symbolic of a deeper transformation:

- **Identity**: Jacob's identity no longer centers on his own strength or cunning but on his relationship with God.

- **Mission**: As Israel, he becomes the patriarch from whom the nation of Israel descends. His calling is elevated from a personal quest for survival to a covenant role that impacts future generations.

- **Divine Ownership**: Biblical renaming often conveys God's sovereign call and claim over an individual's life (e.g., Abram to Abraham, Sarai to Sarah, Simon to Peter). In Jacob's case, it underlines that the blessing he craves is ultimately a gift from a covenant-keeping God.

Symbolic Significance of the Limp: Another outcome of Jacob's nighttime struggle is his permanent limp, caused by the divine being touching his hip socket (Genesis 32:25). In ancient cultures, mobility and physical wholeness were crucial for survival. For Jacob, a patriarch who frequently traveled and had large herds, this impairment was no trivial matter. However, from a spiritual perspective, the limp stands as a perpetual reminder of his encounter with God's grace and discipline.

A limp can be seen as a weakness or vulnerability. Yet the paradox of Scripture is that through weakness, God's strength is perfected (2 Corinthians 12:9). Jacob's limp thus testifies to the transformation that true encounters with God bring:

1. **Dependence**: Every step Jacob takes is now a reminder that God is the source of his strength.

2. **Humility**: The limp prevents Jacob from reverting fully to his old ways of self-reliance.

3. **Obedience**: Bearing the physical mark of the divine encounter, Jacob becomes more inclined to follow God's leading rather than chart his own course.

A Pattern for Spiritual Growth: In evaluating the significance of this encounter for Jacob's spiritual journey, we observe a pattern that can be applied to any believer's path of growth:

1. **Crisis**: Jacob faces an existential crisis, fearing for his life.

2. **Isolation**: He is alone, forced to reckon with God in a place where distractions are stripped away.

3. **Confrontation**: God confronts Jacob's weaknesses, strategies, and identity.

4. **Persistence**: Jacob clings to God, demonstrating both desperation and faith.

5. **Breakthrough**: God blesses Jacob, changes his name, and delivers him from fear.

This cyclical pattern is not unique to Jacob. Many biblical figures, from Moses to David to Elijah, experience analogous processes of divine confrontation leading to transformation. In the New Testament, Peter also undergoes a personal crisis and renaming of sorts. All these accounts highlight God's willingness to meet individuals where they are, yet refusing to leave them unchanged.

Jacob's Reaction and Long-Term Effects: After the encounter, Jacob not only names the place Peniel but also proceeds differently. In Genesis 33, he goes on to meet Esau; the reconciliation that occurs is remarkable and likely beyond what Jacob could have engineered through sheer strategy. This underscores a principle: once we are reconciled with God through an authentic encounter, we often find that God orchestrates reconciliation in our interpersonal relationships as well—though not always immediately or without complications.

Moreover, Jacob's leadership within his family undergoes a shift. While challenges and family strife persist (especially concerning his sons in the later chapters), there is a sense that Jacob leans more on divine promises. The oracles and blessings he pronounces in Genesis 49 reflect a patriarch who is deeply connected to God's purposes, one who has been shaped by a lifetime of divine interactions but especially by that moment at Peniel.

4.3. Who Wrestled with Jacob?

One of the most intriguing questions in the Genesis 32 account is the identity of the being who wrestles with Jacob. The biblical text describes a "man" who appears suddenly in the darkness. Hosea 12:4 refers to this figure as an angel, while Jacob himself proclaims he has seen "God face to face." Traditional interpretations vary:

- **Divine Messenger (Angel):** Some hold that this was a high-ranking angel representing God's presence and authority.

- **Theophany (God Himself)**: Others suggest this was an actual manifestation of God or a pre-incarnate appearance of Christ (a Christophany).

The text itself blends these perspectives. When we read that Jacob calls the place Peniel and states that he has seen God, it pushes the interpretation toward a theophany. However, the mention of an "angel" elsewhere in Scripture cannot be dismissed. In the Old Testament, sometimes "the Angel of the LORD" is spoken of in a way that is interchangeable with God (e.g., Exodus 3:2–6). Thus, it is not entirely contradictory to see this figure as both divine and described as an angelic messenger.

A common Christian interpretation is that the "angel" or "man" was a pre-incarnate appearance of Jesus Christ. This perspective sees such Old Testament appearances of "the Angel of the LORD" as foreshadowings of the incarnation. While the text does not explicitly name Jesus, the principle that "no one has ever seen God" (John 1:18) yet that Christ is the visible image of the invisible God (Colossians 1:15) opens the door to the possibility that these Old Testament revelations were Christ's pre-incarnate manifestations.

Whether or not one adopts this view, the key theological point remains: Jacob wrestled with One who transcended human power and who acted with divine authority. Jacob's own words—"I have seen God face to face, and my life is preserved"—underscore the uniqueness of this encounter.

Why Did God Allow Jacob to Wrestle With Him?: Even if we establish that the mysterious wrestler was indeed God in some form, the question remains: why a wrestling match? Why not appear in a dream, deliver a direct message, or send another vision? Several reasons emerge:

1. **Physicality and Reality**: By wrestling physically, God addresses Jacob's tangible fear and reliance on his own strength. The sweat,

exhaustion, and pain serve as a direct challenge to Jacob's lifelong attempts to control or manipulate circumstances.

2. **A Personal Test**: Throughout the struggle, Jacob refuses to let go, indicating his desperation for God's blessing. God allows the match to continue through the night, illustrating His desire to see Jacob persist and demonstrate genuine faith.

3. **Transformational Moment**: The dislocation of Jacob's hip and the bestowal of a new name become physical and spiritual markers of transformation. A mere vision might not have etched such a lasting, life-altering memory.

There is also the broader redemptive reason: in wrestling with Jacob, God demonstrates His willingness to engage humanity at our level, ultimately pointing to the incarnation of Christ, where God took on flesh and dwelt among us (John 1:14). Jacob's story, then, prefigures the astonishing truth that God is not a distant entity but one who enters into our struggles, meets us where we are, and changes us for His purposes.

The Protective Mercy of a Deliberate Struggle: Interestingly, the text indicates that the wrestling continued until the break of day. One might wonder why God did not instantly overpower Jacob. The simplest answer is that God graciously restrains Himself for our benefit. A single gesture reveals His power to dislocate Jacob's hip, but the prolonged struggle allowed Jacob to come to terms with his own limitations and to cling to God out of necessity.

In a similar way, God may permit prolonged seasons of struggle in our own lives to bring us to a posture of earnest seeking. The Old Testament is replete with examples where God uses extended processes—such as Israel's forty years in the wilderness or Joseph's years in prison—to refine His people's character. The Jabbok wrestling is a microcosm of that principle, teaching that the tension of wrestling with God often births deeper faith and reliance.

4.4. Application for Today's Christians

Wrestling With God in Modern Life: Although few of us will physically wrestle with a divine being, the essence of Jacob's struggle at Peniel remains highly relevant. Many Christians experience seasons where faith feels like a wrestling match with God. Trials, unanswered prayers, and personal crises can create internal friction, leading us to question or challenge God's plans. Like Jacob, we may attempt to control outcomes through our own ingenuity, only to discover that true resolution comes when we submit to God's sovereign will.

Modern examples of "wrestling with God" could include wrestling in prayer for the healing of a loved one, grappling with doubts and questions about Scripture, or battling personal sins and habits that seem impossible to overcome. The story of Peniel reminds us that such struggles, while painful, can lead to profound transformation when we cling to God and refuse to let go.

The Role of Persistent Prayer: In the New Testament, Jesus underscores the importance of persistence in prayer, using parables such as the persistent widow (Luke 18:1–8). Jacob's night-long wrestle exemplifies this principle in the Old Testament. He refuses to release the Man until he receives a blessing, despite the pain. This parallels the idea that believers should persist in prayer, not as an act of defiance, but as a demonstration of faith that God alone can provide the needed breakthrough.

For contemporary Christians, persistent prayer might feel tedious or discouraging, especially when immediate answers are not forthcoming. Yet Scripture encourages believers to "pray without ceasing" (1 Thessalonians 5:17). This doesn't imply vain repetition or striving to manipulate God, but rather maintaining an ongoing posture of dependence, much like Jacob clinging to his divine opponent. Through this persistence, our hearts are often refined, our faith is strengthened, and we are better prepared to receive what God has in store.

Embracing Our 'Limps': One of the most poignant aspects of Jacob's story is that he leaves Peniel with a limp. We, too, may find that profound encounters with God leave us with a metaphorical limp—a reminder of our brokenness, past mistakes, or vulnerabilities. Society often values strength, perfection, and independence, yet Scripture reveals that God's power "is made perfect in weakness" (2 Corinthians 12:9).

When we carry scars or weaknesses from our past—be they emotional, relational, or spiritual—they can serve as testimonies to God's redemptive power. Our "limps" become platforms for ministry, empathy, and humility. Rather than seeing our weaknesses as disqualifications, we can recognize them as opportunities for God to demonstrate His strength. In Jacob's case, the limp was a constant reminder that the blessing he carried was a divine gift, not something he had schemed to obtain. For us, similarly, acknowledging our limitations can make us more reliant on God and more compassionate toward others who struggle.

Identity Change: From "Jacob" to "Israel": Jacob's transformation into Israel has deep implications for believers. The New Testament states that anyone in Christ is a "new creation; old things have passed away; behold, all things have become new" (2 Corinthians 5:17). This parallels the renaming of Jacob: once driven by deceit and self-preservation, now marked by divine purpose.

Many Christians today struggle with labels from their past—be it labels of failure, sin, or personal inadequacy. Yet, the gospel invites us to receive a new identity in Christ. We are called children of God, co-heirs with Christ, and citizens of heaven (Romans 8:17; Philippians 3:20). The story of Jacob encourages us not to let our past or our weaknesses define us. Instead, we are to embrace the name and calling God has for us, living in the reality that, through Christ, we have been redeemed and transformed.

God's Faithfulness Despite Our Shortcomings: A core message of Jacob's life story is that God remains faithful to His promises despite our faults.

Jacob lied, cheated, and manipulated. Yet God's covenant with Abraham extended through Isaac and then to Jacob. At Peniel, God consummates this covenant with a personal, tangible blessing that transcends Jacob's unworthiness. For modern believers, this should instill hope and gratitude. Even when we fall short, God's promises in Christ remain steadfast.

This realization is not a license to live carelessly but rather a motivation for deeper devotion. Recognizing God's covenantal faithfulness invites us to live in thankful obedience, acknowledging that it is God's grace that empowers us rather than our own merit. As the Apostle Paul writes, "while we were still sinners, Christ died for us" (Romans 5:8). This unmatched grace calls us to respond in love, worship, and submission to God's will.

The Necessity of Reconciliation: An often-overlooked aspect of the Peniel encounter is its relation to Jacob's impending reunion with Esau. Before the wrestling, Jacob was consumed with fear, and he tried to manipulate the situation through gifts and strategic division of his family. Yet, after Peniel, his approach to meeting Esau carries a new humility and trust. Remarkably, the two brothers reconcile.

For Christians, this highlights the link between vertical reconciliation with God and horizontal reconciliation with others. Jesus teaches that if someone is offering a gift at the altar and remembers that a brother has something against him, he should first be reconciled to his brother (Matthew 5:23–24). When we wrestle with God and experience His transformative grace, it should lead to a desire to mend broken relationships. We cannot always control others' responses, but personal transformation should at least change our posture, making us more prone to seek peace and forgiveness.

As we reflect on this profound story, let us be reminded that our own transformations are part of God's continuous redemptive narrative. When we find ourselves at our own spiritual "Jabbok," may we cling to the Lord until the break of dawn, confident that He will both bless us and change us for His glory and our good. In the final analysis, the call to "Israel" is the call to let God prevail—turning our struggles into testimonies of His unrelenting grace.

May we, like Jacob, walk away changed, even if we limp in humility. For in our weakness, the strength of God is made manifest, pointing us and those around us to the loving, covenant-keeping God who wrestles with us not to destroy us but to redeem us.

If you found this message encouraging, please share it with others who may benefit. God Bless.

5. Fourth Encounter – In person at Bethel

God reaffirming His covenant and renaming him again.

When we turn to Genesis 35:9-15, we find ourselves in the middle of another crucial turning point in the life of Jacob, the grandson of Abraham and the son of Isaac. At this stage in Jacob's journey, the narrative of his relationship with God has already undergone several transformations—beginning with the remarkable encounter at Bethel in Genesis 28, continuing through his arduous time in Haran with Laban, and then culminating in his decision to return to the land of his fathers. In Genesis 35, we see Jacob revisiting Bethel under God's instruction.

5.1. Purpose of The Fourth Encounter

Jacob, having wrestled with God at Peniel (Genesis 32), reconciled with his estranged brother Esau, and settled for a time in Shechem. But living in Shechem introduced new complications for Jacob's family. His daughter, Dinah, was dishonored there, and her brothers, Simeon and Levi, sought vengeance in a brutal way (Genesis 34). Their violent retaliation risked endangering Jacob's entire household, as it sparked the potential for retribution from surrounding peoples.

In response to these dangers and to further align Jacob's heart with God's will, the Lord commanded Jacob to return to Bethel, the very place where He had first revealed Himself through the famous ladder dream (Genesis 28). Bethel held significant meaning for Jacob; it was where God initially confirmed the covenant promise that He had given to Abraham and Isaac. Therefore, returning to Bethel was not merely a geographical relocation—it symbolized a spiritual redirection and reaffirmation. God called Jacob back to his roots of faith, reminding him of the promise and the presence that accompanied him on his earlier journey.

Renewing the Covenant and Transforming Identity: In Genesis 35:9-15, we see a clear divine intention: God seeks to reconfirm and emphasize Jacob's identity as "Israel" and to remind him that he is part of the unfolding plan that began with Abraham. The text states that God appeared to Jacob again in Bethel and re-affirmed: "Your name is Jacob; your name shall not be called Jacob anymore, but Israel shall be your name" (Genesis 35:10). We note that the name change from "Jacob" (which can mean "supplanter" or "heel-grabber") to "Israel" (often understood to mean "God fights" or "one who struggles with God and prevails") had already occurred during the wrestling match at Peniel in Genesis 32. Yet here in Genesis 35, God reinforces that change in identity. This isn't merely a reiteration of a prior event; it is God's way of telling Jacob, "I am serious about who you are now, and I am serious about the covenant I have with you."

Hence, one core purpose of the Fourth Encounter is to declare Jacob's new identity firmly in the presence of God. Humans are forgetful creatures; the repeated emphasis reminds Jacob of who he is and the spiritual authority he is to walk in. He is no longer to be primarily defined by his old patterns of deception and manipulative behavior. Instead, he is to live out the reality of being God's covenant partner—an identity that calls him to holiness, trust, and reliance on divine direction.

Additionally, in verses 11 and 12, God reiterates the Abrahamic covenant: "I am God Almighty: be fruitful and multiply. A nation and a company of nations shall proceed from you, and kings shall come from your body" (Genesis 35:11). The language here calls back to the original mandate given to humanity in Genesis 1:28 ("Be fruitful and multiply"), and especially to the covenant made with Abraham in Genesis 17. By restoring Jacob to Bethel, God is effectively stating that Jacob's family has not disqualified itself despite sins and failures. The covenant is still in place; the promise remains sure. The impetus is on Jacob to step into that covenantal promise in a manner consistent with his new identity.

The Message of the Encounter

First and foremost, it's a message of God's unwavering faithfulness. By the time we reach Genesis 35, Jacob has accumulated quite a history—one that includes deceit, fear, triumph, family conflict, and remarkable blessings. Through all these episodes, God remained faithful, honoring the promise He made to Abraham, extending grace upon grace toward Jacob, and ensuring that Jacob's destiny was aligned with God's redemptive plan. Jacob's story often mirrors our own journeys, where we experience failures and successes, yet God remains consistent in His character and faithful to His word.

Secondly, there is a powerful message of transformation. Jacob's name change to Israel underscores that the old ways of deceit and self-reliance must give way to a life of faith and surrender to God's will. This transformation cannot be seen as merely a superficial label; it implies an inward renewal and a call to walk in alignment with God. Every Christian who reads this passage can glean the lesson that when God calls us by a new name—whether that be "child of God," "beloved," or "redeemed"— He expects us to walk in accordance with that new identity. Our past mistakes do not define us when God speaks His promises into our future.

Lastly, the message includes God's desire for worship and remembrance. In Genesis 35:14-15, Jacob sets up a pillar at Bethel and pours out a drink offering on it. This act demonstrates reverence, gratitude, and a willingness to commemorate the place where God appeared to him. In the Old Testament context, pillars and altars often served as physical memorials of God's intervention in the life of His people. They helped individuals and communities remember what God had done. In our modern context, we may not set up literal stone pillars, but the principle remains the same: we mark the moments when God meets us, rescues us, speaks to us, or transforms us, so that we will never forget His goodness and will pass on these testimonies to others.

The Structure of the Encounter

One way to see the purpose of this encounter is by examining the structure of Genesis 35:9-15. This passage can be outlined as follows:

1. **God Appears to Jacob Again** (v. 9): This emphasizes continuity with the past encounters. God is consistent and never abandons His covenant partners.

2. **Reiteration of the Name Change** (v. 10): A second reminder that Jacob's identity has changed. God is highlighting the significance of the transformation that Jacob experienced.

3. **Renewal of the Covenant Blessing** (vv. 11-12): God uses language reminiscent of the Abrahamic covenant, reminding Jacob of his place in a grand narrative that includes fruitfulness, dominion, and the promise of land and legacy.

4. **Jacob's Response in Worship** (vv. 14-15): Jacob erects a pillar and pours out offerings as a tangible expression of reverence and obedience.

No matter how many times Jacob (or we) falter, God calls us back to the place of promise and the posture of worship.

5.2. Spiritual Significance

When Jacob first encountered God at Bethel, he was a lone fugitive fleeing from the wrath of his brother, Esau. He vowed that if God took care of him, he would return to Bethel and worship. Now, decades later, Jacob arrives with a large family, servants, and abundant possessions. This marks not just a physical return but a spiritual coming of age. Through hardships, successes, and revelations, Jacob grows from a fearful trickster into the patriarch Israel, capable of guiding an emerging nation.

Spiritually, this transition signifies maturity. Early in his life, Jacob often relied on deceit and human cunning to secure blessings. By the time he returns to Bethel in Genesis 35, his posture is one of reverence. He leads his household in purging their idols, building an altar, and publicly affirming God's place of honor. The significance lies in witnessing how personal encounters with the divine—when he fled from Esau, when he was under Laban's scrutiny, when he wrestled at Peniel—now culminate in a settled, worshipful recognition of God's sovereignty over every aspect of his life.

Affirmation of God's Character: At the core of this fourth encounter is a profound affirmation of who God is—faithful, merciful, and steadfast in His covenant. The significance is not just in what Jacob receives, but in what Jacob learns about God. Throughout his life, Jacob witnesses God's protection, provision, and patience, culminating in this moment at Bethel where God reiterates the same promises, demonstrating that nothing—neither Jacob's flaws nor the failures of his family—can thwart God's plan.

This affirmation of God's character underscores that every divine encounter in Jacob's life serves a dual purpose: instructing Jacob about God's nature and inviting him to reflect that nature in his own relationships. For today's believers, recognizing the significance of this passage means understanding that each encounter with God in Scripture reveals facets of His grace, justice, and covenant-keeping faithfulness.

Jacob's Response as a Template for Believers: Ultimately, Jacob's response—removing idols, building an altar, and pouring out offerings—demonstrates humility and devotion. It highlights a template for believers throughout the ages:

- **Repentance:** Jacob cleanses his household of foreign gods, a symbol of turning away from sin.

- **Reverence:** He acknowledges the sacredness of Bethel by building an altar, symbolizing the seriousness with which he approaches God.

- **Remembrance:** He sets up a pillar as a perpetual memorial of God's revelation, teaching future generations to recall the mighty works of the Lord.

- **Renewal:** He embraces the reaffirmation of his new name (Israel), committing himself anew to the divine calling on his life.

Each of these actions forms a pattern for genuine spiritual transformation. Genuine encounter should prompt a renunciation of sin, heartfelt worship, remembrance of God's deeds, and a renewed commitment to follow God wholeheartedly. The significance of Jacob's fourth encounter at Bethel, therefore, reaches beyond ancient patriarchal history to instruct believers on how they, too, might respond to divine grace. Jacob's transformation echoes through time, reminding us that every encounter with God invites a deeper commitment and a more profound recognition of His covenant faithfulness.

5.3. Who Revealed to Jacob?

In Genesis 35:9-15, the text indicates that "God appeared" to Jacob, while earlier encounters sometimes reference "the Angel of God" or "the Angel of the LORD." The best biblical and theological reasoning indicates that in many of these pivotal encounters, the being described as "the Angel of the LORD" is actually a direct manifestation of God—what theologians call a theophany—or even a preincarnate appearance of Christ (a Christophany). The reason for this mode of revelation lies in God's desire to engage with humanity intimately, yet in a form that would not overwhelm or destroy them —God revealing Himself in a tangible, accessible form to human beings.

A natural question arises: why would God appear in angelic form or as a human figure rather than as an overpowering, unveiled deity? In Scripture, direct encounters with God in His full glory often lead to fear, trembling, and even the possibility of death (Exodus 33:20). By veiling His glory in human-like or angelic form, God offers a merciful accommodation, allowing people to interact with Him without being consumed by His holiness. This principle aligns with the theological concept of God "condescending" or stooping down to humanity's level for the sake of relationship and revelation.

Response to the Encounter: Jacob's reaction in Genesis 35 appears more subdued than in Genesis 32, where he wrestled through the night and walked away with a limp as a perpetual reminder of that encounter. Here in Genesis 35, he sets up the pillar and offers worship. However, the text does not describe Jacob exhibiting alarm or terror. Perhaps his prior experiences had prepared him. He understood that this was the same God who had previously encountered him in dreams, who had wrestled with him by the Jabbok River, and who had guided him out of Laban's household. By now, Jacob recognizes the voice and the authority. Thus, Jacob's primary response is one of worship and submission, indicating that he is coming into greater alignment with God's will.

5.4. The Personal Application for Today's Christians

The same God who interacted personally with Jacob desires to shape our identities, draw us into covenant relationships, and lead us to a place of worship and consecration. Below, we explore a few key areas of application that arise from Jacob's experiences.

Returning to Our "Bethel": Jacob was initially called to Bethel in his youth when he was fleeing from his brother Esau. At that time, Bethel became a place of promise. Years later, after a season of trials, conflicts, and victories, God called Jacob to return to Bethel. This physical journey mirrored a spiritual renewal—a returning to the foundational place of encounter and commitment.

For modern believers, "Bethel" represents those pivotal experiences where God first revealed Himself to us. It might be the moment of our salvation, a powerful worship service, a retreat, or a season of intense personal transformation. Over time, busyness, sin, discouragement, and the pressures of life can dull the memory of that initial calling and enthusiasm. Jacob's example reminds us of the importance of periodically "returning to Bethel," meaning intentionally revisiting and nurturing our foundational experiences with God. This can involve personal retreats, extended times of prayer, or engaging in corporate worship with a renewed hunger for God's presence. The purpose is not to live in the past, but to rekindle the flame of devotion, remember God's promises, and realign our priorities to His will.

Embracing Our New Identity: Jacob's name change to Israel serves as one of the most compelling illustrations of personal transformation in Scripture. Once labeled a deceiver, Jacob was re-labeled as Israel—a name signifying wrestling with God and prevailing by God's grace. Christians, too, receive a new identity in Christ. When we are born again (John 3:3), Scripture says we become new creations (2 Corinthians 5:17). We are no longer defined by our old patterns of sin or by worldly standards of success or failure. Instead, we are called "children of God," "co-heirs with Christ," and "a holy priesthood" (Romans 8:17; 1 Peter 2:9).

70

However, just as Jacob struggled to fully live out his new name, we often wrestle with unbelief, guilt, or the lingering influence of old habits. Jacob's repeated reaffirmation by God at Bethel shows us that embracing our new identity is a process that requires repeated encounters with God's grace. We need to be reminded—through the Word, through fellowship, and through prayer—of who God says we are. In practical terms, this can manifest in daily declarations of biblical truth, cultivating an atmosphere of worship that feeds our faith, and participating in discipleship relationships where we hold one another accountable to our new identity in Christ.

Removing Idols and Consecrating Ourselves: Before heading to Bethel, Jacob instructed his family: "Put away the foreign gods that are among you, purify yourselves, and change your garments" (Genesis 35:2). This was an act of preparation, acknowledging that encountering God's holiness demands reverence and a turning away from idolatry. In our modern context, idols may not take the form of carved images, but we can still harbor "foreign gods" in the form of misplaced priorities, materialism, unhealthy relationships, or addictions that claim our ultimate loyalty instead of God.

Applying Jacob's directive to our own lives means examining our hearts for anything that hinders our devotion to Christ. This examination might include assessing how we spend our time, money, and emotional energy. Are there "idols" like career ambition, social media, or even ministry itself that have taken a place in our hearts that belongs to God alone? Once identified, these idols must be laid down as a clear act of repentance and consecration. Much like Jacob told his family to "change their garments," we may need to change our behaviors and external commitments to reflect an internal, renewed focus on God. Repentance and consecration are not singular events but ongoing practices that keep our hearts aligned with God's purposes.

Trusting God's Faithfulness Despite Our Failures: Jacob's story is marked by lapses in faith, deception, and familial dysfunction. Yet, in Genesis 35, God once again establishes the covenant with him. This underscores a central gospel truth: God's faithfulness supersedes our failures. As Christians, we can sometimes fall into the trap of believing that past sins or current struggles disqualify us from God's promises. Jacob's life testifies that while consequences may still unfold from our actions, God's ultimate plan and gracious purposes can and do prevail.

This is not a license for complacency or sin, but rather an assurance that genuine repentance and returning to God never result in rejection. When we stumble, we can confidently approach God's throne of grace (Hebrews 4:16), trusting that He will restore, discipline in love, and reaffirm His promises to us. In practical application, this means not allowing regret or shame to prevent us from seeking God. Instead, like Jacob, we rise, return to Bethel (that place of grace and promise), and receive anew the assurance of God's covenant love.

Spiritual Leadership in the Home: Another relevant takeaway from Genesis 35 is Jacob's role in directing his household to purify themselves and put away foreign gods. By doing so, Jacob exercised spiritual leadership, guiding his family toward a collective act of worship. In today's Christian context, parents, guardians, or anyone entrusted with leadership roles in families or small groups can learn from Jacob's example. Spiritual leadership isn't just about personal holiness; it involves fostering an environment where others can also encounter God.

This might look like regular family devotions, honest conversations about faith, or setting priorities that honor God above all else. Leading by example means demonstrating repentance, humility, and genuine love for God. Ultimately, the spiritual well-being of those entrusted to our care can be significantly influenced by our willingness to guide them toward seeking God wholeheartedly and removing whatever idols may hinder that pursuit.

Expecting Transformative Encounters with God: While not everyone will have a dramatic theophany, the principle that God desires personal encounters with His people holds true today. Prayer, worship, the study of Scripture, and fellowship are avenues through which we can experience God's transforming presence. Jacob's life shows that encounters with God are not one-time events but can recur at crucial junctures, guiding and reshaping us.

For believers who may feel spiritually stagnant, the story of Jacob encourages openness and expectation. Are we asking God to meet us in fresh ways? Are we positioning ourselves—through spiritual disciplines and an obedient heart—for new revelations of His character and will? A posture of expectancy allows us to discern God's voice more clearly and to be ready for the transformation that such encounters inevitably bring.

Holding Fast to Covenant Promises: When God reaffirmed the covenant to Jacob at Bethel, He connected Jacob to promises that extended far beyond his immediate circumstances—promises that would shape the destiny of an entire nation. Christians, too, live under a covenant—the New Covenant established by Christ's blood (Luke 22:20). This covenant promises forgiveness of sins, the indwelling of the Holy Spirit, and eternal life (Jeremiah 31:31-34; John 3:16).

In a world that bombards us with uncertainties, remembering the surety of this New Covenant brings hope and stability. Whether we face personal crises, societal unrest, or spiritual doubt, we can anchor ourselves in the knowledge that God has pledged Himself to us through Jesus Christ. Jacob's experiences show that God consistently upholds His end of the covenant, even when we waver. Let us, therefore, cling to these covenant promises, letting them shape our worldview, our decisions, and our hope for the future.

Lessons in Perseverance: Jacob's journey was lengthy, filled with setbacks and breakthroughs. The Fourth Encounter at Bethel didn't mark the end of his challenges—he would face the death of Rachel, the loss of Joseph (believed to be dead), and other family complications. Yet, the reaffirmation at Bethel fortified him with a renewed sense of God's presence and purpose. This teaches us that divine encounters and reaffirmations of faith often prepare us for further trials, rather than exempting us from them.

For Christians, perseverance is a vital aspect of discipleship. James 1:2-4 reminds us that trials refine our faith, producing perseverance and maturity. The encouragement from Jacob's life is that these hardships never occur apart from the covenant grace of God. When we return to our Bethel moments—to the promises God has spoken—we find the strength to endure and even to grow in faith.

A Call to Worship and Remembrance: Ultimately, Jacob's response to God's appearance at Bethel was worship. He commemorated the event with tangible offerings and established a pillar as a permanent reminder. Worship is not merely a religious duty; it is the heart's response to the magnitude of who God is and what He has done. For Christians, the call to worship is equally compelling. In every season—whether we are celebrating blessings or walking through valleys—we are invited to lift our eyes to the One who remains faithful.

Regular corporate worship (in church gatherings) and personal worship (in daily devotions) become channels through which we realign our hearts with God's purposes. As we worship, we re-encounter the God who met Jacob at Bethel, the God who changes names, restores broken lives, and unfolds His redemptive plan across generations. Worship, then, is both a privilege and a responsibility, a way of ensuring we never lose sight of the covenant promises that define us.

In conclusion, in Jacob's Fourth Encounter at Bethel, we see the culmination of a journey that involved deceit, reconciliation, and ultimately transformation into the man God had called him to be. The personal applications for Christians today are abundant. We, too, must return to our "Bethel" moments to refresh our faith, embrace our new identity in Christ, remove idols, build altars of remembrance, and persevere through life's trials anchored in God's covenant faithfulness.

What God did for Jacob—meeting him personally, reaffirming His promises, and giving him a new name—He continues to do for believers in Christ. Our lives, like Jacob's, are weaved into a grand narrative of redemption, one that spans from ancient patriarchs to the present day. As we cling to the lessons gleaned from Jacob's story, may we experience our own Bethel encounters that revive our hearts, shape our destiny, and bear testimony to the unchanging faithfulness of our covenant-keeping God.

If you found this message encouraging, please share it with others who may benefit. God Bless.

APPENDIX I. Jesus Christ: The True Ladder Between Heaven and Earth

In Jacob's dream (Genesis 28:10–22), the ladder linking heaven and earth served as a powerful symbol of God's ongoing communication and covenant with humanity. However, in the fullness of time, Christians see this symbol as pointing toward Jesus Christ, who declared Himself the ultimate mediator between God and humanity. "And he said to him, 'Truly, truly, I say to you, you will see heaven opened, and the angels of God ascending and descending on the Son of Man'" (John 1:51). This section explores how the dream at Bethel foreshadows Christ and how Jesus fulfills and surpasses the imagery of Jacob's ladder.

Old Testament Foundations

Jacob's Ladder as a Symbol of Connection: Jacob's ladder is a tangible representation that God is intimately involved in human affairs. It bridges the gap between the divine and the earthly realm, suggesting that the covenant people of God are under continual angelic oversight and that

God Himself stands sovereign over them. This resonates with the broader Old Testament theme that God dwells among His people, whether in the Garden of Eden, the Tabernacle, or the Temple. The ladder in Jacob's vision is thus one more instance of God's abiding presence and promise.

Foreshadowing the Need for a Mediator: The patriarchal narratives often highlight the distance between a holy God and sinful humanity. Throughout the Old Testament, various figures serve as mediators or intercessors: Moses acts as a mediator of the Mosaic covenant, priests offer sacrifices, and prophets deliver God's word. Jacob's ladder anticipates the ultimate necessity for a mediator who will permanently unite heaven and earth. This is partly why many scholars see Jacob's dream as a precursor to the grander revelation in Christ.

Jesus Christ as the Fulfillment of the Ladder

Jesus as the Son of Man: In the Gospel of John. Chapter 1, Verse 51, Jesus references Jacob's ladder after meeting Nathanael. He says, "…you will see heaven opened, and the angels of God ascending and descending on the Son of Man". By invoking the imagery of Genesis 28, Jesus is making a profound statement about His identity and mission. He is, in essence, the "ladder" by which angels traverse, the axis mundi that unites the divine and human realms. Jesus was declaring Himself not merely as a teacher but as the pivotal point of contact between heaven and earth.

Christ: Fully God and Fully Man: The theological foundation for Jesus functioning as this "ladder" is tied to the doctrine of the Incarnation. Jesus is fully God and fully man (John 1:1, 14; Philippians 2:6–8). Because of His divine nature, He has direct access to heaven; because of His human nature, He shares in our earthly existence. Therefore, He alone can reconcile God and humanity. This dual nature is the ultimate fulfillment of what Jacob's ladder symbolized: an unbreakable link between the divine sphere and the human realm.

Reconciliation Through the Cross: While Jacob's ladder functioned as a vision of God's presence and promise, Christ's work on the cross is the actual mechanism of reconciliation. The apostle Paul explains, "For in him all the fullness of God was pleased to dwell, and through him to reconcile to himself all things... making peace by the blood of his cross" (Colossians 1:19–20). The cross, therefore, can be seen as the real "ladder" or "bridge" that reconciles sinners to a holy God. Jesus' reference to angels ascending and descending on Him suggests that all spiritual blessings, including angelic ministries, flow through the person and work of Christ.

The Implications of Christ as Jacob's Ladder

Direct Access to God: Under the Old Covenant, access to God's presence was limited to specific times, places, and people (e.g., the High Priest entering the Holy of Holies once a year). In Christ, the veil of the temple is torn (Matthew 27:51), granting believers direct and continual access to the Father (Hebrews 4:14–16). Jesus Himself teaches, "I am the way, and the truth, and the life. No one comes to the Father except through me" (John 14:6). The imagery of the ladder is fulfilled in Him, who gives unfettered access to heavenly blessings.

Perpetual Mediation: Christ's role as mediator did not cease with His ascension. The book of Hebrews emphasizes that Jesus lives to make intercession for believers (Hebrews 7:25). Unlike the dream-ladder that Jacob saw for one night, Jesus' mediation is continuous and everlasting, ensuring that believers are always under His grace and guidance.

Heavenly Citizenship: By uniting heaven and earth in Himself, Jesus also grants believers a new identity: citizenship in heaven (Philippians 3:20). While Jacob awoke to realize that the place he slept was "the house of God," Christians live in the reality that their bodies are temples of the Holy Spirit (1 Corinthians 6:19). They are perpetually in the presence of God because Christ, the eternal ladder, has made a dwelling place in their hearts.

Mission to the World: If Jesus is the link between heaven and earth, the Church's mission flows from that reality. Believers, as members of Christ's body, are called to be ambassadors, extending the kingdom of God on earth as it is in heaven. This parallels the ascending and descending angels, who minister and execute God's will. In union with Christ, Christians participate in this heavenly mission, bringing the good news to a broken world.

The Ladder Imagery in Early Christian Writings

Patristic Interpretations: Church Fathers such as Irenaeus, Augustine, and others often interpreted Old Testament stories in light of Christ. They saw in Jacob's ladder a foreshadowing of the Incarnation—God becoming man to raise humanity up to God. They would preach that the ladder's foot on earth and top in heaven prefigured Christ's birth on earth while remaining one with the Father in heaven. Such an interpretation underscores how the early Church viewed the unity of the two Testaments, with Christ as the key to understanding the Old.

Medieval and Reformation Insights: In medieval Christian thought, the ladder sometimes symbolized spiritual ascent through prayer, sacraments, and virtue, all made possible by Christ's mediation. During the Reformation, Protestants like Martin Luther and John Calvin emphasized Christ's unique role as the sole mediator, viewing the ladder as an image of grace rather than human effort. Thus, any "ascent" to God comes only through faith in Christ's finished work, not by works of the law or human merit.

Personal Application: Living in the Reality of the True Ladder

Confidence in Prayer: Because Jesus is the ladder, believers can approach God with confidence. The writer to the Hebrews exhorts, "Let us then with confidence draw near to the throne of grace" (Hebrews 4:16). This confidence stands in stark contrast to Jacob's initial fear and wonder.

While awe is still appropriate, believers have a deeper assurance, knowing that the One who unites heaven and earth intercedes for them personally.

Assurance of Salvation: Jacob woke up from his dream unsure about the future, but God's presence reassured him of divine promises. In Christ, believers have an even firmer foundation for assurance. Paul writes, "There is therefore now no condemnation for those who are in Christ Jesus" (Romans 8:1). This security stems from Christ's role as the permanent "ladder," guaranteeing that nothing can separate believers from the love of God (Romans 8:38–39).

Motivation for Holiness: Recognizing that Christ is the bridge between heaven and earth should inspire believers to live holy lives in response. The apostle John remarks, "And everyone who thus hopes in him purifies himself as he is pure" (1 John 3:3). If Jesus has opened the heavenly realms to believers, then their everyday conduct should reflect their heavenly citizenship, maintaining integrity, love, and purity as testimonies of God's kingdom.

Engagement in God's Mission: The angels ascending and descending are on a mission, performing tasks in service of God's will. In the new covenant context, believers partner with Christ in bringing the gospel to the nations (Matthew 28:19–20). As branches connected to the true vine (John 15:5), Christians partake in extending divine grace, mercy, and truth, bridging the gap for others who do not yet know Christ. This underscores the missional dimension of seeing Jesus as Jacob's ladder: He is the only way to salvation, and the Church is called to proclaim this good news.

In Conclusion, Jesus Christ stands at the heart of the Christian faith as the true and living ladder between heaven and earth. While Jacob's dream provided a revelation of God's covenant presence and a foreshadowing of divine-human union, Jesus' Incarnation, death, and resurrection accomplished the reality that Jacob's ladder symbolized. Believers now have uninterrupted access to the Father through the Son, and they are invited to live in the power of that connection every day.

The dream at Bethel thus converges with the message of the gospel: God seeks a covenant relationship with His people, providing access to His presence and fellowship. By declaring that the angels ascend and descend on the Son of Man, Jesus unequivocally identifies Himself as the focal point of all God's dealings with humanity. The ladder Jacob saw in a fleeting vision is an eternal reality in Christ, bridging our earthly struggles with the heavenly promises of God. Therefore, Christians can rejoice, worship, and serve with the assurance that in Christ, heaven is open, and God's grace flows freely into the hearts of those who believe.

If you found this message encouraging, please share it with others who may benefit. God Bless.

APPENDIX II. The Angel of the Lord: More Than a Messenger

In various Old Testament passages, there appears a mysterious figure known as "the Angel of the Lord." This being speaks with divine authority, receives worship, and at times is identified interchangeably with God. While Genesis 28 references angels and the Lord standing above the ladder, it is part of a broader biblical pattern where the line between an angelic messenger and God Himself can blur. This section dives deeper into the significance of "the Angel of the Lord," exploring why this entity is more than a mere messenger and how it connects to the dream at Bethel.

Biblical Appearances of the Angel of the Lord

Hagar's Encounter (Genesis 16:7–13): The Angel of the Lord appears to Hagar in the wilderness, comforting and guiding her. Hagar refers to this figure as "the God who sees me," indicating she understood this angel to be a manifestation of God's presence. The text often alternates between "the Angel of the Lord" and "the Lord" in describing who is speaking.

Abraham's Sacrifice of Isaac (Genesis 22:11–18): As Abraham prepares to sacrifice Isaac, the Angel of the Lord stops him. This figure again speaks with divine authority, providing a substitute ram and reiterating the covenant blessings. The language used suggests a direct equivalence between God and His angel.

Moses and the Burning Bush (Exodus 3:2–6): The text states that "the Angel of the Lord" appeared in a flame of fire out of the midst of a bush. Yet, as Moses approaches, God calls out to him, saying, "I am the God of your father, the God of Abraham, the God of Isaac, and the God of Jacob." This passage is a primary example of the Angel of the Lord speaking and acting as God Himself.

Gideon's Commission (Judges 6:11–24): The Angel of the Lord appears to Gideon, calling him a "mighty man of valor" and commissioning him to deliver Israel from the Midianites. The text again alternates between "the Angel of the Lord" and "the Lord," culminating in Gideon's realization that he has seen God face-to-face.

Theological Interpretations of the Angel of the Lord

A Theophany: One view is that the Angel of the Lord represents a theophany—a manifestation of God in a tangible form. Since no one can see God in His unmediated essence and live, these appearances serve as God's condescension to human limitation. This perspective aligns with passages where the angel receives worship, something regular angels refuse (cf. Revelation 19:10, 22:8–9). If the Angel of the Lord accepts worship and speaks as God, it indicates that this figure is not a created being but God revealing Himself in a veiled manner.

A Pre-Incarnate Christophany: Another widely held Christian interpretation is that the Angel of the Lord is a pre-incarnate appearance of the Second Person of the Trinity, Jesus Christ. Since the New Testament identifies Jesus as the "image of the invisible God" (Colossians 1:15) and "the radiance of the glory of God" (Hebrews 1:3), it would not be inconsistent to see the Son as the manifestation of God in Old Testament times. This view gains further support from the fact that after the Incarnation, the specific title "Angel of the Lord" no longer appears in the New Testament, suggesting that the true "Messenger of the Lord" had come in human form.

Connecting the Angel of the Lord to Jacob's Dream

Standing Above the Ladder: In Genesis 28:13, "the Lord stood above it and said…" This statement could align with the pattern seen in other theophanies where "the Angel of the Lord" is used interchangeably with "the Lord." While the text in Genesis 28 does not explicitly say "the Angel of the Lord," its structure—mentioning angels first, then the Lord speaking—reflects the broader motif of God manifesting His presence in contexts where angels are involved.

Jacob's Later Wrestle (Genesis 32): Jacob's later encounter at Peniel, where he wrestles with a mysterious "man," is often interpreted as a theophany. Hosea 12:3–4 clarifies that this was an angelic being who found Him at Bethel, also Jacob names the place Peniel, meaning "the face of God." This continuing thread strengthens the case that the "man" or "angel" could be God Himself in some form. Thus, the "angel" in these episodes with Jacob is no ordinary messenger; he exhibits divine qualities and authority.

The Ongoing Revelation of God's Nature: The interplay between angels and God in Jacob's life reveals how the narrative gradually unveils the nature of divine revelation. The figure that appeared above the ladder did more than convey a message; He engaged Jacob directly in covenantal promises, something only God could do. In subsequent biblical history, this pattern of the Angel of the Lord revealing God's presence prepares readers for the ultimate revelation in Christ.

Significance of the Angel of the Lord's Identity

Affirms God's Relational Nearness: The fact that God appears in a form that humans can interact with underscores His desire for a relationship. Whether one interprets these appearances strictly as theophanies or Christophanies, the takeaway is that God chooses to relate to His people in a personal way.

Highlights God's Authority and Sovereignty: The Angel of the Lord speaks with the full authority of God, demonstrating sovereignty over human affairs. Jacob's dream emphasizes this aspect, as God (or His angelic manifestation) stands above the ladder, sovereignly directing angelic activity.

Foreshadows the Incarnation: Many Christian theologians see in these appearances a foreshadowing of the Incarnation, where God would ultimately become flesh in Jesus Christ. The ladder in Jacob's dream points to the need for a divine-human mediator, and the Angel of the Lord's recurring appearances hint at God's plan to directly dwell among His people.

Maintains the Holiness of God: By appearing in a veiled form, God safeguards His holiness. After all, no sinner can behold God's essence without consequences. The Angel of the Lord thus allows a real encounter with God while preserving the necessary distance that God's holiness demands.

While the Angel of the Lord played a key role in revealing God's presence under the Old Covenant, the New Testament makes clear that Jesus surpasses these manifestations. The writer of Hebrews states, "In these last days he has spoken to us by his Son" (Hebrews 1:2). Therefore, Christ is the ultimate revelation, the true and final way God has chosen to reveal Himself and to commune with humanity.

In Conclusion, the Angel of the Lord represents a unique category in biblical revelation—often interchangeable with God, receiving worship, and executing divine judgment or deliverance. This figure thus transcends the role of a mere heavenly envoy. In Jacob's dream, the angels' presence on the ladder and the Lord's position above it reflect the same kind of transcendent-yet-imminent dynamic seen in other appearances of "the Angel of the Lord." It signals that God Himself is presiding over the affairs of His people, bridging heaven and earth in a profound way.

For Christians, these events pave the way for understanding Christ's identity as the ultimate revelation of God. They also reinforce the truth that God is not confined to the heavenly realm but actively involved in the lives of His covenant people. When we read about the Angel of the Lord, we see glimpses of the divine humility and love that would find its fullest expression in the Word becoming flesh. Thus, the Angel of the Lord stands as a scriptural signpost to the Incarnate Son, reminding us that God has always been, and will always be, "God with us."

If you found this message encouraging, please share it with others who may benefit. God Bless.